Managing Britanni

If the Socialism is Authoritarian; if there are
Governments armed with economic power as they are
now with political power; if, in a word, we are to have
Industrial Tyrannies, then the last state of man will be
worse than the first.

Oscar Wilde, *The Soul of Man under Socialism*, 1891

Management, like the emperor's clothes, does not exist;
the prime myth of management is that it does.

Robert Heller, *The Naked Manager for the Nineties*, 1995

Managing Britannia

Culture and *Management*
in *Modern Britain*

*

Robert Protherough
and John Pick

ia

Paperback published in 2003 by Imprint Academic
PO Box 200
Exeter EX5 5YX
UK

Copyright © 2002 The Brynmill Press Ltd
First published in 2002 by The Brynmill Press Ltd

ISBN 0 907845 53 3

A full CIP record for this book is available from the British Library.

typeset in Garamond

Contents

Acknowledgements   *page* vi
Preface   vii

1   The Cultures of Management   9

2   How Managers Behave   29

3   The Language of Modern Management   47

4   Management as an Academic Subject   69

5   Managing the Arts   95

6   Managing the Schools   117

7   Managing the Deity   141

8   Rebranding Britain   155

9   The Real World: Management in Literature   173

10 Bursting the Managerial Bubble   191

Index   207

Acknowledgements

In the course of this book's preparation, we have benefited from many helpful discussions with colleagues and students, both in and out of formal classes. Our thanks are also given to Paul Bissen and Adrian Seville, who suggested material and sources, and to Ben and Jane Roberts for their critique of the book's main argument. We owe a special debt to Judith Atkinson and Caroline Gardiner, who read chapters in draft and made many helpful comments, and to Ian Robinson, for the detailed interest he has taken in every stage of the book's production. However, we alone are responsible for the opinions expressed in the text and for any factual errors which it may contain.

Robert Protherough, John Pick   2001

Preface

In the 'eighties we began to be seriously alarmed by a
number of things that were happening in British education, amongst them the fact that "management" was
being taught and promoted as a skill which could readily be
detached from the people and processes that it was managing.
At that time each of us was separately writing about the
swelling tides of bureaucracy which seemed to be engulfing
the universities, churches, schools and the administration
of the arts. Everywhere there seemed to be a concern with
presentation rather than substance, and in the way things
were being managed there was an increasing emphasis on
numerical targets and less and less attention given to the
ways management affected people.

A decade later things were getting decidedly worse, for it
seemed that all of our previous worries were now dangerously merging into one. A sinister new orthodoxy, to which
we later attached the term "modern managerialism",
seemed to be spreading into every part of Britain. No
British institution—cathedral, college, hospital or arts
centre—was safe from it. Soon it was being openly asserted
that "in the modern world" every aspect of life—
hospitality, friendship, eating out or caring for one's family—
had to be *managed*, with managerial "targets" set for each
part of its operation, and with league tables tabulating
successes and failures.

Yet this was not management as we had once understood it. The new managerialism was wholly based on
quantifiable data, and dealt largely in symbols and ab-

stractions. British culture was itself turned into an "industry" and rendered down to columns of statistics. The public services were now given "targets" to achieve, like steelworks in the former Soviet Union. Everything, including so-called assessments of quality, was now commodified and judged quantitatively. And those blessed with managerial qualifications became the most desireable commodities of all. As managers hopped from one kind of business to another, they gained the sort of golden handshakes and salaries that put them in the same financial league as professional footballers.

It seemed to us that all this was both foolish and harmful. It was foolish to have so many intelligent people squandering their talents on such trivialities, and harmful because the machinations of modern managerialism were steadily undermining and destroying art, scholarship, religion and much else that had made life in Britain worth living. We decided that a warning was needed, and that was the spur to write this book.

It could have been twice as long. Material showing the ravages wrought by this new managerialism has crowded in upon us, and of necessity we have had to leave out a number of the bizarre happenings that might have further illustrated our argument. For the same reason we have not expanded upon the significance of the way in which organisations concerned with the arts, education, religion and the social services are now regularly retitled and reorganised—not for reasons of principle, but because it suits the managerial bureaucracy. Instead we have simply called public services and commercial enterprises by the title they had at the time of writing, and left our readers to draw their own conclusions about the curious fact that the Department of Education and Science, for example, having for a brief spell been the Department for Education and Employment, is now the Department for Education *and Skills*. . .

I

The Cultures of Management

It is generally agreed that the development of management, as a discrete business practice and as an academic subject, began with the publication of Frederick Winslow Taylor's third book, *The Principles of Scientific Management* in 1911. Winslow Taylor advocated that men of commerce should pool their traditional business knowledge, reduce it to laws and formulae, and produce a "science of management". Scientifically-trained managers could then take over the organisational skills which were being wastefully dissipated throughout the workforce, and the production and marketing of goods would become more efficient as a result. Winslow Taylor's work thus marks the beginning of a transition from a time when fewer than 1% of those involved in business bore the title of managers, to the modern world in which no business is thought to be properly run unless at least 15% of its workforce is, one way and another, managerial. It also records the first stirrings of that modern cult, which was to grow apace during the last decades of the twentieth century, which accords managers a venerated, near-divine status. For the success of an enterprise no longer depends upon the quality of the goods and services it may offer, but upon the value which the jobs market puts upon its management team. *Managers* are now held to be the one indispensable element in any business or service. If a firm's productivity

9

falls, or its products fail to sell, its shop floor workers will be unceremoniously laid off. By contrast its managers will rarely be dismissed, and when they are, they will be appeased by handsome gifts.[1] More probably their numbers will be enlarged, for failing businesses are now commonly conceived to be in need of more rather than better management, and in need of ever more wordy advice from the managers' expensive allies, the ubiquitous *management consultants*.

It was in America that management first took root. As Robert R. Locke observes in his recent study of American management, it was the Americans who "invented management and with it the American way of doing business".[2] The academic study of management became established in the USA when the first MBA course was offered in 1916 at Columbia University, but it was the 1920s which saw the first substantial growth in the study of the new "science"—with Wharton, Harvard and then the Michigan School of Administration offering MBAs. Now there are more than 700 MBA programmes in the USA, where study at a business school offers a near-guarantee of a lucrative managerial career. It is for example estimated that a typical graduate of Harvard's 1974 MBA programme will now be contemplating early retirement, having amassed a fortune of more than $8 million.[3]

Not until the 1960s did the study of management spread to these shores. American-style MBA programmes were then established in the universities of London and Manchester, in defiance of those who warned that far from

1 Jennie Page, sacked as Chief Executive of the Millennium Dome a month after its disastrous opening, was awarded a "golden handshake" of more than £150,000. Lord Birt, who chose to leave the BBC three months before the end of his contract, was for his final year given a sum of £1,500,000, which combined salary, bonuses and a golden handshake. This represented, over the five years of his contract, a payment increase of 1,000%. His financial position was further eased when he was awarded a lucrative contract to write a book on (how could we have thought otherwise?) management.

2 Robert R. Locke, *The Collapse of the American Management Mystique*, Oxford, 1996, p. 29

3 John Micklethwaite and Adrian Wooldrige, *The Witch Doctors*, 1997

underpinning the growth of the national economy and thus shaping the national culture, the supposed new "science" of management was itself a cultural manifestation. For, as Locke remarks: "Management is an American term and an American creation. Although American management has always hankered for universality, it is nothing more than a cultural peculiarity."[4] Since then the study of management in Britain has spread steadily, until it is just about the only subject area which its universities have in common. There are currently around 12,000 students studying on Britain's 120 MBA programmes, and in many modern universities the Business School is the fastest-growing and best-resourced faculty.

It will be a recurrent theme of this book that management is now applied to realms far removed from production industry, and to realms where it has, by any sensible reckoning, no business. There is scarcely any part of our domestic and social experience which is not now described by our politicians as an *industry*, so that its problems can be presented as mere problems of production, marketing and sales, and therefore capable of solution only by *managers*. Our cathedrals and our country-side are seen as resources to be packaged for the "Tourist Industry". Eating out is the concern of the "Hospitality Industry". Caring for the sick is now part of the production line processes of the "Health Industry". The modern poet is no longer just a writer; he or she is a product of the new "Creative Industries", a product awaiting profitable exploitation.[5] And Britain's rich cultural history is itself repackaged as a commodity, to be valued only for its profitability, for as Sir Neil Cossons, chairman of a neo-governmental organisation called English Heritage, has recently remarked, "This government has no

---

4 Robert R. Locke, *op. cit.*, p. 1

5 The present Poet Laureate, Andrew Motion, was in many quarters admired for selling his *Millennium Eve* poem to the *Mail on Sunday* for a handsome sum.

antipathy to heritage. They just want to know what the
return on the investment is."[6] Indeed the government feels
so confident of its ability to "manage" the national culture
that it produced, in March 2001, a Green Paper prescribing
the national culture for the following decade. *Culture and
Creativity: The Next Ten Years* showed that the government
had a much greater faith in its ability to manage the output
of "creativity" than in its ability to manage more tangible
concerns   such   as   the   London   Underground,   car
production or the care of livestock on the farms. But then,
modern   management,   like   modern   government,   is
increasingly concerned with fashioning attitudes, and less
and less concerned with tangible goods and services. In the
run-up to the 2001 General Election, Peter Mandelson
thought it perfectly proper to say that in its second term
the New Labour government should be "about inaugur-
ating a new age of ambition in our country, weaving
together the rightful quest for material affluence with a
deeper striving for better relationships . . .".[7] And it was
entirely in keeping with the new managerialist times that
the late Princess Diana should have announced in a
Panorama interview that her personal troubles, which had
previously seemed to have other causes, in fact stemmed
from a lack of proper managerial targets. At the time of
her marriage, it appeared, she had not been given a proper
business plan. "No one sat me down with a piece of paper,"
she complained, "and said, 'This is what is expected of
you'."

Of course only a fool would deny that human affairs
need to be organised, that businesses need to be run, and
services efficiently maintained. In all walks of life there is
need, amongst other things, for careful husbandry, a need
to set attainable goals, to maintain standards and to satisfy
demands—in a word to do the things which our craftsmen
and our housewives, our farmers and cooks, our butchers,

6 *The Times,* 3 April 2000   7 *The Sunday Times,* 6 May 2001

bakers and candlestick makers have done for centuries. Rightly we honour the memory of managers such as Jesse Boot, Dr Barnardo, Florence Nightingale, Thomas Cook, the Joseph Rowntrees or W. H. Smith—people who have in past times created and run great and purposeful enterprises. But we do not admire them because of their excellence as personnel officers, resource controllers, production co-ordinators, relocation directors, downsizers or marketers—indeed they would not have understood the meaning of most of those terms—but because of the distinctive skill, dedication and prowess showed by each of them within their very different realms. It is the *differences* between them which help to define each one's particular genius. The notion that they had in common a single talent which can be identified as "managerial skill", capable of ready transference between their different callings, is pure fantasy. That Dr Barnardo could equally well have run a chain of newsagents, or that Thomas Cook could just as readily have run a chocolate factory, is manifestly absurd.

Yet the modern world believes as fervently in the *transferability* of management as it believes that management skills are separate and identifiable realities. Managers of supermarket chains can nowadays expect to be head-hunted for posts in national museums; managers of finance companies or high-profile television performers can expect to be offered high-level managerial positions in our universities. Whereas Dr Barnardo dedicated his whole life to caring for destitute children, involving himself fully in every part of the process from raising funds to bathing orphans, the directors of Britain's modern charities—the salaries of the hundred largest now average in excess of £80,000 a year—are recruited from managerial roles in commerce, the City, the armed forces, retailing and insurance, and perforce keep their distance from the work on the ground. They do not need to know at first hand anything about the distress which their charity is ostensibly set up to alleviate. Their duty is to solicit financial support, to invest their resources prudently,[8] to recruit and motivate staff, to meet externally set "targets" and to produce businesslike company reports. The management of a modern charity is thus about as different from the work of Dr Barnardo as it is possible for it to be.

The belief in the transferability of managerial skills is so piously maintained that advertisements for modern managers, while scrupulously detailing the desired "managerial skills", are often vague about what is actually in need of management. Consider the main text of an advertisement which appeared in *The Observer* (12.12.99):

> [This key role] manages corporate planning and performance processes within a Best Value framework to drive business improvement.
>
> Operating at a strategic level, the successful applicant will be required to manage the Corporate planning function and a performance review framework, including Best Value and developing key systems processes to support this legislation will be a key part of the role.
>
> We are seeking someone with proven organisational skills combined with a sound working knowledge of the requirements of Best Value and performance management. Excellent leadership skills are essential alongside the ability to influence and advise at board level.

The significant thing about this (wholly typical) text is the way in which conventional, even mundane, office routines are repackaged as high-definition managerial skills. There is plainly little merit in actually understanding the function of the enterprise—that which is (according to the advertisement) to be planned, processed, driven, strategised, managed, reviewed, developed, legislated,

---

8 It is now more than ever necessary to appoint managers of charities for their financial acumen than for their concern for the poor and needy. From 1999 charities have been permitted to invest more than 75% of their total assets in equities.

organised, worked, led, influenced and advised about—as the actual function of the organisation is seemingly incidental to its effective management. Does it perhaps manufacture garden fertilizer? Operate as a Sixth Form College? Sell surgical equipment? In the event it is hardly surprising to learn that it does none of these things. The advertisement was for a "Head of Corporate Development" for the Hertfordshire Police Force.

The term "management", in little more than half a century, has thus radically changed its meaning. When Winslow Taylor was advocating that it strive to become a science, management meant something reasonably straight-forward, like "the efficient organisation of available resources". Some management was clearly necessary, but the most senior people in any field were not usually its managers, but its leading professionals. Activities of many kinds—the work of doctors, teachers, architects and pig farmers, for instance—involved some management, but professional skills and judgement overrode such merely functional aspects, and were superior to them. Managers knew their place. The farm manager sowed and harvested the crops the landowner decided upon. A ward manager carried out the instructions of the senior surgeons. A theatre manager made sure that everything ran smoothly in the staging of the director's chosen programme.

In the 1960s, when politicians of all parties seemed united in their belief that Britain's primary aim must be to become more "competitive" and so richer, the traditional codes and practices of the professions began (rather oddly) to be linked with "Britain's besetting sin", *amateurism*. The way to becoming more competitive was by employing in senior positions more and more magic "managers", who were able, unlike ordinary mortals, to bring us "into the second half of the twentieth century". By 1980 it was being asserted, as a self-evident truth, that "the management ethos must run right through our national life—private and public companies, civil service, nationalised industries, local government, the National Health Service".[9] It became axiomatic that every part of British life, from the police forces to children's homes, must be run, not as in the sinfully amateur times of old, by experienced professionals who had worked their way up through their respective fields, but by one of the new breed of all-purpose "managers". But as these modern managers talked and thought in their own enclosed managerial jargon, they could converse neither with professionals in the field nor with their specialised workforce, so they naturally sought the companionship and support of others of their kind. This is one reason why modern managerialism inevitably spawns fast-breeding bureaucracies. We have quickly become accustomed to that alliance, and it is not uncommon for the bureaucratic "management" of an organisation to take on a life of its own and smother the organisation it is supposedly managing. Thus it no longer surprises us to learn that when members of the Law Society in the mid-'nineties complained that they were getting poor service for their annual membership fee of £245, the management replied that as much of their 800 staff members' time, and most of their £55 million budget, was spent in *managing* the Society's affairs—particularly in servicing the Society's 160 active committees—there were inadequate resources remaining to deal with such marginal issues as the members' *legal* enquiries.

Such managerial bureaucracies are now to be found in government, in the City, the Church, the multinationals, the armed forces, the universities, the business corporations and every sector of public life. In the first five years of Mrs Thatcher's National Health Service reforms (1989–1994) the number of NHS administrative staff rose by 18,000, while in the same period the number of nursing

9 Michael Heseltine, "Ministers and Management in Whitehall", in *Management Services in Government*, H.M.S.O., 1980

staff fell by 27,000. After seven years of Lord Birt's recent restructuring of the BBC, managers had doubled in number, by then comprising some 26% of the 24,000 staff, so that when in 2000 his Lordship left the BBC, basking in the warm congratulations of the Prime Minister, an independent auditor (July, 2000) found that the BBC management was overstaffed by some 1,100 people and was needlessly wasting £130 million a year of licence payers' money. After three years of similar restructuring the Arts Council of England and its regional satellites were shown, on a similar audit, to have increased their bureaucracies by 30%. Nor are auditors themselves without sin. The National Audit Office spent some £311,000 on its own "management consulting services" in 1987–8, a figure which by 1995–6 had increased tenfold to £3,619,000.

This was not what the gurus of the new managerial "science" had forecast. In 1988 Peter Drucker had confidently announced that within twenty years the numbers of managers employed would fall by two thirds, and that the business organisation of the future would bear little resemblance to the traditional company:

> Instead it is far more likely to resemble organisations that neither the practising manager nor the management scholar pays much attention to today: the hospital, the university, the symphony orchestra. For, like them, the typical business will be knowledge-based, an organisation composed largely of specialists who direct and discipline their own performance through feedback from colleagues, customers and headquarters.[10]

We hear much less, now, of the administrative savings the "knowledge-based economy" will bring us, and rather more about its escalating bureaucratic costs.

As the dividing line between public and private sector has become blurred, their managerial practices have

10 Peter Drucker, *Harvard Business Review*, Jan/Feb 1988

merged. Hospitals and universities have become more like overstaffed multinational companies. Public services are now frequently led by imported private sector managers, who reorganise them unsuitably into competing "cost-centres", the operation of which needlessly occupies many bureaucratic hours. In their turn private businesses are increasingly "aided" by new forms of government invest-ment and then policed by state spies in the guise of public or consumer *watchdogs*. Thus bureaucratic control over every kind of business transaction has greatly increased. The "privatised" national railway system, which receives from government an annual subsidy of approaching £2 billion (a larger grant than was formerly given to the "nationalised" system), has now more bureaucrats engaged in assessing its development than it has train drivers and platform porters. In like fashion it costs tax-payers around £400 million a year to have what might have been thought to be the heart of the "knowledge-based economy", the British universities, assessed for their managerial competence.

One result of this cross-infection of public- and private-sector values is that the distinction between government and management, once clearly understood, has over the last thirty years been gradually lost. In the nineteenth century it was believed both in the USA and in Britain that the best government was that which governed least—although not everyone would have gone as far as Thoreau in asserting "that government is best which governs not at all"[11]—and that government should not only stay out of private and family affairs, but should so far as was possible, stay out of commerce and private business. In the 1960s it was still perfectly respectable to believe with R. A. Butler that politics was "the art of the possible", that good government did not involve the total *management* of every aspect of our lives but rather the

---

11 Henry Thoreau, *Civil Disobedience*, Washington, 1849

organisation of those realms in which governments had legitimate power to make effective change. But in the modern world there are no bounds to what governments think they can shape and manage. Modern governments now affect to be able to manage everything, from how ambitious we are, to how fat women should be.[12]

Neither the commodification of the national culture, nor the belief in the limitless power of management, is a wholly new phenomenon. "It was already being suggested sixty years ago that the collapse of capitalism would be brought about not by the uprising of the proletariat but by a rising class of powerful managers who would themselves become a new ruling class."[13] (The managerial revolution will be complete when managers use the power of the state to consolidate their position.) And culture was already considered by government to be a saleable commodity in the 1970 White Paper, which advocated Britain's full entry into what was at first called the Common Market, then the European Economic Community and finally, when its bureaucracy had grown to monstrous proportions and its political ambitions had swelled accordingly, simply "Europe". It was in this publication that the importance of industrial growth over every kind of cultural consideration was first offered as a moral imperative to the British people. Britain's cultural history, as a part of the old Europe, was now deemed infinitely less important than the hoped-for trade benefits with the new European Union. According to the Short White Paper (para.8) economic progress was that "which we all desire". For "Britain lives by trade", and its economic strength was the only quality by which it could now be judged. Cultural boundaries must be ignored

12 Tessa Jowell, the Blair Government's "Minister for Women", proposed at a government "Body Image Summit" in June 2000 that the present generation of young women should be liberated "from the tyranny that their mothers and grandmothers have felt" to be too thin. This was to be achieved by government managers "monitoring" the shape of women depicted on television and in the press, and "issuing guidelines".

13 James Burnham, *The Managerial Revolution*, New York, 1997

in the shared desire for material riches, for "The differences
between European neighbours are insignificant, compared
with what we have in common." (White Paper para. 32).

Common sense did not however desert all those in
public life. As late as 1972, a report entitled *The New Local
Authorities; Management and Structure* (produced in the wake
of the 1971 Maud Report's "rationalisation" of the administration of the British counties) was still proclaiming the
long-held distinction between private sector management
and the operation of public services:

> Changes in management structure or process must
> be justified in terms of the benefit to the community,
> for in the last analysis it is to the community that local
> government is accountable. In the business world
> management relates to the maximisation of profits; in
> local government management is about, and more
> important for, people. (2:13)

Yet the report spoke defensively, as if aware that any such
distinction must soon be lost. Its alarm over those who
wished to blur the boundaries between public service and
commerce was cautiously expressed:

> Local government may well have lessons to learn from
> industry, but one must be wary of attempting wholesale
> transplants from one to the other. To pursue the
> analogy, the rejection factor will be extremely high
> because of the different nature of the constraints within
> which management must operate in the two fields. (2:5)

In the event, their apprehension was well justified, for it
was almost the last time the essential difference between
public administration and commercial management was
expressed in a public report. The old notion of "public
service" was soon to be discredited as a form of
"amateurism". A decade later the public services were
being repackaged in the neo-industrial trappings of
Thatcherism and brought under the computerised control

of modern management. Their financial systems were "rationalised": their results were thenceforward efficiently "delivered" and they met "targets". They no longer offered service but became "accountable" to "clients" and in everything they offered "value for money"—that is they worked for cash and for no other purpose. As David Farnham and Sylvia Horton remark, the process of repackaging was thorough and sometimes brutal:

> These new managerialist orientations across the new public services have been introduced by a variety of means, including political imposition, propaganda and changing public service cultures.[14]

Thus Mrs Thatcher ushered in the first British "managerial state", which used the language of free-market enterprise but which was at centre state-controlled. In the new managerialism the remaining barriers between governing and managing were finally breached.

And so the new state "industries" were born, coagulates of activity which were not, as the old nationalised industries had been, wholly funded by government, but were instead wholly *managed* by it, being set targets, monitored and evaluated by eager new packs of government watchdogs. Some new state "industries", like the rail network, were created from a former nationalised industry. Others, like the "agriculture industry", were herded together from the private sector. Still others, like the "creative industries", seemed to exist only in the heads of state bureaucrats. Direct government spending (and with it, personal taxation) was reduced by the expedient of selling off and "privatising" many of the former public assets—a sale of council houses was followed by the privatisation of gas, electricity, telephones, water and, finally, the railways. But in the meantime *indirect* government spending on the new managerial bureaucracies

14 David Farnham and Sylvia Horton (eds), *Managing the New Public Services*, 1993

grew mightily. In 1979, the year Mrs Thatcher came to power, indirect spending on government quangos (quasi-autonomous, neo-governmental organisations) by government amounted to £114 million. Twenty years later the quangos—now retitled "non-departmental public bodies" (NDPBs)—were annually spending £16,950,000,000 of taxpayers' money, together with a further £1,700,000,000 of Lottery money and a further £3,200,000,000 from other sources—altogether over one hundred times as much.

The older quangos, including the BBC, the British Council and the Arts Council of Great Britain, had operated on the understanding that their governance would be by unpaid board members drawn from a spectrum of political interests. There existed in British life a rule of political etiquette known as the "arm's length principle", which meant that such organisations were granted a degree of autonomy in their affairs, and parliament generally kept its distance. But after Mrs Thatcher's election that changed abruptly. Those quangos which survived were now crammed with the Prime Minister's supporters—by the mid-'eighties the BBC governors, for the first time in their history, had both a Conservative chairman and a Conservative vice-chairman. Members of such bodies were usually now paid. As successive layers of these neo-governmental bodies were brought into being, their function changed. In the jargon of the day, they became "proactive"; no longer independent and advisory in nature, but agents of government and regulatory in function. They were there to set targets, monitor the new *industries* and direct government investment, in a word to function much as the old USSR's middle management had functioned, as the eyes and ears of the state. The "arm's length principle" became a thing of the past. William Rees-Mogg spoke its epitaph when he announced in a public lecture that under his chairmanship the Arts Council had instead become "the government's arm" for managing the arts.[15]

The widespread adoption of modern management techniques rested upon two beliefs: that everything, from eating habits to team games, should (and *could*) be regulated and managed by the state, and that in every realm of national life it was possible for quantitative targets to be set and achieved by managerial action. As neither of these propositions could for long be rationally sustained, it became imperative for governments also to practise another, complementary, form of "management". The manipulation of political *facts* and of public opinion became essential adjuncts to modern management practice. Older and straightforward words for such deception, such as propagandising or mass-marketing, were gradually sidelined, and newer terms—"consumer awareness" and "issuing guidelines"—adopted to give the process a warm and friendly feel.

Setting the right industrial "targets", and the publicising of their achievement, became as important in modern Britain as it had been inside the old Soviet Union. And in those cultural realms where excellence had formerly lain in quality, quantitative targets became the norm. Thus museums were no longer to be judged by their curatorship, but by the ethnic mix of the public they attracted. Schools were assessed less by the education they offered than by their achievement of quantitative state "targets". In the new climate, the emphasis moved to manipulating the way services were *perceived*, rather than letting their tangible accomplishments speak for them. Whether it was over street muggings, food safety or the reliability of its transport systems, Government spin-doctors could always use their own statistics to convince the public that they (the public) thought that things were improving, and politicians could therefore insist that, in the vacuous phrase of the last big British Rail publicity campaign, "We're getting there."

15 William Rees-Mogg, Arts Council Lecture, 1986

In 1995 Dr Hoggart discussed the changes wrought by Tory governments and wrote that "Better times may bring back better practice".[16] Yet the auguries were not good. Even as Dr Hoggart was expressing his hopes, the shadow cabinet was being compulsorily dispatched on a special course at Somerville College, Oxford to study (what else?) modern management. And once in office Mr Blair's government exceeded his predecessors' passion for managerial bureaucracy by creating a new NDPB or "task force" on average once every six days. Government reliance on managerial target-setting and spin-doctoring increased, and the distinction between government and management became more blurred than ever. The new government soon had Ministers ostensibly "responsible" for whole swathes of experience which realistically they could neither govern nor manage, such as "Youth", "Women", "Sport" and the forces of "Change". On the other hand more tangible matters in which government could sensibly intervene, such as drug-taking, homelessness or the functioning of H.M. Prisons, were increasingly made the responsibility of managerial "Tsars"— accountable to Ministers but not to parliament or people.

And the *industrialisation* of every part of British life continued apace. Sir Richard Wilson's report on *The Future of the British Civil Service* (1999) for example suggested that the Civil Service could be restructured as an *industry*, with top managerial posts thrown open to outsiders, with the government laying down its industrial targets, with productivity bonuses for all employees, staff quotas of women and "representatives of the ethnic minorities". These improvements would naturally be monitored by a neo-governmental watchdog authority, which in its own words would be a "Public Service Leaders Scheme, talent-spotted to target under-represented groups without losing market appeal."[17]

16 Richard Hoggart, *The Way We Live Now*, 1995, p. 287
17 Try as they will, the authors cannot make any sense at all of this important-sounding statement.

In short Mr Blair's first government took to itself a far greater degree of centralised managerial control than any of his peacetime predecessors had done. This was said by New Labour apologists to be in response to a threatening entity called "globalisation", an apparently malign amalgam of the new information technologies with modern economic forces. But Mr Blair raised another spectre, even more terrifying than globalisation. That was the force of "change". "Change" was the great elemental force in the new managerial universe. We had to submit to "change" or be destroyed. For Britain's cultural history had, in New Labour's view, neither moulded us as a nation nor had it prepared us for "change"; indeed, it had left us little better than brute beasts.[18] Other post-war governments may have urged the British to rid themselves of some outdated imperialist attitudes, but Mr Blair's government was the first to claim that the British were totally incapacitated by their own history:

> We all know this is a world of dramatic change. In technology; in trade; in media and communications; in the new global economy refashioning our industries and capital markets; in family structure; in communities; in life styles.
>
> Add to this the change that sweeps the world, the changes that Britain has seen in the 20th century—the end of Empire, the toll of two world wars, the reshaping of our business and employment with the decline of traditional industries—and it is easy to see why national renewal is so important.
>
> The choice is: to let change overwhelm us, to resist it, or equip ourselves to survive and prosper in it. The first leads to a fragmented society. The second is pointless and futile, trying to keep the clock from turning. The only way is surely to analyse the challenge of change and to meet it.[19]

18 In July 2000, the Home Secretary, Jack Straw, suddenly suggested that British football hooligans were impelled to behave in the way they did because of "their imperial past".
19 Tony Blair, Speech to the CBI Annual Dinner, 1998

The spurious sense of crisis which this evokes, the rhetoric of "national renewal", linked with the insistence that there is no alternative, is a curiosity when the Prime Minister is addressing a prosperous and peaceful nation. Yet the manufactured sense of urgency—as if there had never before, in all its long history, been a risk of Britain becoming "a fragmented society", and as if nothing which Mr Blair were now doing to its history, language and culture could possibly be furthering that process of fragmentalisation—is crucial to Mr Blair's purposes. He wants to say that we are both imperilled and yet offered salvation by the forces of "change", *and that only a society totally possessed by the spirit of modern management can possibly control and manage such primeval forces.*

So every possible resource is mobilised and trained for the struggle. Every part of British life is regimented into new *industries* so that it may come under the new managerial control, and earn New Labour's favoured accolade as being truly "modern". Old values, be they in religion, public welfare, the arts or education, are set ruthlessly aside. In November 1999, with hopes for a revival of liberal education almost extinct, and those traditional university departments which remained chronically short of funds, an announcement was made that the Treasury was committing an extra £68 million over five years to a major new Institute of Management, to be jointly run by Cambridge University and the Massachussets Institute of Technology. This, rather than the traditional university, would equip Cambridge to meet the challenges of modern "change".[20] In May 2001 the government made it clearer still that they regarded the universities as nothing more than industrial commodities, boosting the GNP of "Great Britain Plc". They announced the creation of yet another university, this time in Cornwall, to which they were initially committing £30 million. The Trade Minister

20 *The Times*, 9 November 1999

spelled out the government's reasons: "The government is committed to harnessing the intellectual property of every region, and universities have a vital role to play in local economies."[21] It must alarm us that such crassness—once rare in British public life—can now be so casually and so shamelessly displayed.

21 *The Independent*, 8 May 2001

2

How Managers Behave

Of course things must be managed, and it therefore still seems to many people that modern managers are engaged in a necessary and rational pursuit. Indeed, faced with questions about resources, production or marketing, they do appear to behave much as their forebears did— establishing the basic facts, analysing the nature of the problem, weighing up alternative strategies and then coming to managerial judgements. Yet we shall demonstrate that what they are actually doing is quite different from what was formerly meant by "managing" something. We shall then show that not only is much modern management superfluous, but that the behaviour of its disciples is widely destructive, fuelled as it is by an obsessive and irrational belief in the "reality" of a fictive, wholly-manageable universe. Although the way our public services and some of our private industries are currently being managed is worrying enough, when a government announces that it is setting out to increase the sum of national "creativity", that it is "committed to harnessing the intellectual property of every region" or that it intends quantitatively to raise the nation's level of "ambition", *and thinks that it can achieve those fantastical ends by the application of modern management techniques*, then something has gone seriously wrong.

On the face of it, modern management does not seem to differ much from traditional practice. All management decisions need to some degree to be informed by facts, and there can hardly ever have been a society more relentlessly dedicated to advertising "facts" about itself than is modern Britain. The country's citizens are subjected to increasing numbers of government surveys, which it is now a crime to ignore.[1] They are spied upon by more than 500,000 CCTV cameras as they drive or shop. 100 million of their telephone calls can be monitored each week from GCHQ's headquarters in Gloucestershire, while at the Menwith Hills Signals Intelligence Base in Yorkshire computers can scan millions of their private e-mails at random every day. Meanwhile data collection has become an "industry" in its own right, and managers and management consultants can now buy "facts" to fit every managerial process. They can for example arm themselves with the knowledge that in 1999 the average Briton spent 215 minutes each day watching television, or the fact that in 1997 each visitor to a British gallery spent on average three seconds in front of each artwork—seven seconds less than in 1987—or even purchase the information that precisely 58% of adult British men believe in aliens.[2] Quasi-governmental organisations regularly publish catalogues of state-approved facts for the new managerialism, with titles like *Social Trends, A Map of the Creative Industries* or *Facts About The Arts.*

It is here that one begins to notice that these facts are not—as facts once were—a *part* of the process of modern management, providing a means of better analysing a managerial problem, or of better informing a business strategy. To all intents and purposes they *are* the managerial process. They contain within them both the presumptions

1 The 2001 British Census form, much lengthier than its predecessors, perfectly exemplified the new managerialism, from its convivial headline "Count Me In!", implying that completing it was a matter of friendly choice, down to the footnote, in much smaller type, explaining how the state could punish you if you didn't fill it in to their satisfaction.

2 These "facts" are from a useful anti-"fact" diatribe, David Boyle, *The Tyranny of Numbers*, 2001

that the remedy for any kind of cultural malfunction must lie in more modern management, and that managerial action alone will produce the desired results. Consider, for example, the way in which the education authorities in Hull have reacted to the fact that their schools are regularly bottom of one of the government's school league tables:

> Hull—bottom of the national GCSE league tables for the past four years—is to pay for headteachers to attend management courses in an attempt to improve the city's image and raise educational standards.
>
> The authority has written to all 104 of the borough's schools asking if they want to study for a masters degree in business administration. . . .
>
> "We want the best possible people to come to Hull and while we don't have a problem filling headships, we do want to improve the quality of the people applying," said a spokesman.
>
> "We are hoping that by offering headteachers the chance within a certain number of years to qualify as an MBA, we can use the course as a marketing tool." A trip abroad—possibly to Tennessee—to see how overseas schools operate will be one of the attractions on offer.[3]

As disciples of modern management, the Hull authorities naturally believe that the educational, cultural and moral problems in their schools' performance can be smoothed away by considering them in purely managerial terms, as matters of "image" or "marketing". And of course they also believe that a little judiciously-applied management training will simultaneously raise the level of teacher applicants, improve the pupils' performance, and burnish Hull's international reputation. It does not occur to the managerialist mind that such action could, possibly, make things even worse.

Yet what is certain—and what may just possibly worsen things—is that the Hull headteachers will, as their

3 *The Times Educational Supplement,* 25 May 2001

managerial studies increasingly occupy them, have less direct contact with their staffs and with their pupils than they had before. For maintaining a distance from that which is being managed is a key component of the modern managerial process. The achievement of modern managerial goals generally involves a high degree of mental abstraction, but little direct contact with the organisation's workers, with the production of its goods or services, or with its customers and users. As the admirable Professor Mintzberg says in his most recent book, in the course of a discussion on the miseries of airline travel,[4] most modern managers are ". . . capable of manipulating symbols and abstractions, but ill-equipped to deal with real decisions involving people and difficult dilemmas—to manage, in a word." With the result that, in spite of all the management training, customer service is, according to Mintzberg, getting worse all the time.

A quarter of a century ago, the same writer was already noting important changes in managerial behaviour. In a pioneering study of the way chief executives actually came to their decisions,[5] he noticed that they did not behave in the conventional business school manner. They took little account of independently-produced information. They spent comparatively little time analysing or diagnosing managerial problems, but instead tended to react rapidly and intuitively, according to increasingly abstract managerial formulae, and without considering anew the interests of workforce or customers. That process is now much further developed. Twenty-five years ago it would have been almost unthinkable for "management" to be considered separately from what was being managed, as cookery could not be imagined as an activity distinct from its ingredients and kitchen utensils. Now management is thought to be a wholly self-contained mode of behaviour,

4 Henry Mintzberg, *Why I Hate Flying*, Texere, 2001
5 Henry Mintzberg, *The Nature of Managerial Work*, New York, 1973

governed by its own universally applicable axioms. The result is that the management of universities, theme parks, supermarkets, record companies and railway tracks[6] is in modern Britain all of a piece.

Whereas different managements were once closely identified with their products—Palethorpe's Sausages, Reckitt's Dyes, Colman's Mustard—commercial enterprises now buy and sell managers like big football clubs buy and sell their players. And whereas one might once have employed a manager because he was likely to improve the product, better motivate the workforce and hence make and sell more, nowadays a manager is employed because of his or her fabled ability to deal with such abstract matters as "long-term strategy", "market positioning" or "rebranding", which should be at best only a small part of a responsible manager's range. For when they become the *entirety* of the managerial process, such abstractions anaesthetise managers from feeling direct responsibility for workers or customers, or to the public at large. The manager's priorities then lie within a notional universe rather than in the real world. For example, when managers are "creating a range" they are pursuing a conceptual notion rather than producing useful things which meet real needs; when they are "processing orders" they are concerned with something much less tangible than merely pleasing customers, and when they are involved with "making strategic alliances" they are engaged in a process which seems altogether more abstract than the production of ordinary goods and services:

> Nutravida, another health and beauty retailer, was launched in November 1999 with funding of just £1 million, a rather modest sum during those "easy money" days.
>
> By September, the site was struggling after failing to

6 The new chief of Railtrack had previously been head of a private coal mining company.

raise more, which founder Trevor Millett blamed on an "appalling" market "in terms of buyer interest".

"We went into a mode which we called 'silent running' while we looked for a suitable partner," says co-founder Peter Brockbank. "Silent running" involved sacking its fifteen employees and sharply cutting monthly expenditure.

Nutravida's first step to recovery was a trading alliance with a shop in Chiswick, west London, called Apotheke 20-20. Customers can still shop online using the Nutravida website while Apotheke 20-20 holds the stock and processes orders. The website is almost breaking even and sales are increased by almost 20% per month, according to Brockbank, now Nutravida's only full-time employee.

He is close to a deal with a mail order company which will create an own-label range of Nutravida products to be sold in shops and online. "The only way to make a dotcom operation work is by making a strategic alliance with another party," says Brockbank.[7]

In the jargon-ridden world of the new technologies, struggling to counter "change", adrift in so much virtual reality, it is easy to forget the fifteen people who were dismissed from their jobs when the firm went into "silent running mode", and easier still to ignore the interests of flesh-and-blood customers.

It is moreover hard to imagine how Nutravida's manager and sole employee actually behaves when he is "managing". For what do you look like, sound like or even *smell* like when you are in the throes of making "a strategic alliance"? Once it was easy to describe managers at their work: Wedgwood anxiously touring his workshops, Rolls discussing the new suspension systems with Royce, Bertram Mills impetuously betting a friend that he *could* put on a circus at Olympia in a few months' time. By contrast modern management is almost impossible to observe as it

7 *The Daily Telegraph*, 22 March 2001

is taking place, and its essence seems to lie in putting a favourable gloss on already-completed actions. As with some parts of modern physics, it is sometimes possible to trace the consequences of managerial action but not to describe the event itself. We can hardly ever say, "Look, *there* is somebody managing!" So descriptions of modern managers in action dwell upon the supposed consequences of the managers' behaviour, rather than attempting to describe the actions which led to them—with the result that the people in the descriptions seem curiously unreal, and imbued with strangely magical powers like characters in comic strips:

> Matthew Freud, people say, is the most well-connected [*sic*] man in London, and therefore the country at large. . . . He says he doesn't want to be the story, but nowadays there are no stories, only news management and media manipulation, that's the story. At the turn of the millennium, we are all aware that spin makes the world go round. That's why the man behind the man has become such an intriguing and potent symbol of our times . . .
>
> He worked tremendously hard during . . . the Eighties, networking furiously, without great rewards. One former girlfriend claimed that he could speak to three people on the phone, in three different accents, with three different spins, "While simultaneously having sex with me."[8]

An earlier age, with different superstitions, might well have accused Mr Freud—here speaking in tongues as he pleasures his familiar—of practising witchcraft. We view him much more indulgently. The superhero status, the symbolic importance so readily accorded him, the mumbo jumbo used to describe the arcane rituals in which he is indulging, the general air of illusion and wizardry and the fact that according to this description his behaviour

8 *The Observer*, 16 January 2000

appears to be quite unrelated to the production of any tangible goods or services, mark him out as the epitome of modern management in action.

It was not ever thus. Managers in the nineteenth century—who also had to combat technical innovation, no less disturbing in its way than the "change" with which our government constantly threatens us—were able to react imaginatively to events, show managerial judgement and foresight, and produce tangible benefits for their workers and their customers or users. This for example is how one mid-nineteenth-century entrepreneur described the opportunities provided by one contemporary "change"—the development of the railways in Victorian Britain:

> Amongst the varied agencies now at work on the minds and morals of men, there are few more powerful than Railways and Locomotion. The opening of a railway in an ignorant and barbarous district is an omen of moral renovation and intellectual exaltation. The prejudices which ignorance has engendered are broken by the roar of a train of carriages, and the whistle of the engine awakens thousands from the slumber of ages.[9]

However exaggerated such observations may now seem, the managerial *action* which Thomas Cook then decided upon, and executed, was firmly rooted in the everyday world. Cook's first step in management—the running of a teetotal railway excursion on 5 July 1841 from Leicester to Loughborough—was imaginatively conceived but thoroughly down-to-earth in its execution. It attracted a solid show of public support:

> In the morning a large body of excursionists, variously numbered at 570 and 485, gathered at Leicester station. They were accompanied by temperance officers and a uniformed brass band, and watched by a crowd some two or three thousand strong. Marshalled by Cook, they

9 *Cook's Excursionist*, June 1854

climbed on board one second-class carriage and nine "tubs", the open, seatless carriages in which third-class passengers travelled during the early days of rail, and set off on the eleven-mile journey. Every bridge along the line was thronged with spectators and when the train arrived in Loughborough it was greeted by a crush of temperance supporters and onlookers.[10]

Cook's business grew rapidly, until it became a "global" company—but it continued to be based on an imaginative awareness of the possibilities for the new "tourism", coupled with an intensely practical understanding of matters of detail. A successful commercial transaction was impossible for him without real concern for the welfare of his staff and customers. For Cook "customer service" was never an abstraction. And his reporting of his own work was without the self-indulgent "spin" of modern managerial reporting, which makes his own commentary on his achievements the more telling. As he wrote towards the end of his hugely successful career, he had always tried to make his work "remunerative as well as publicly beneficial; and we have yet to learn, that there is anything . . . hostile to true philanthropy in commercial success."[11]

Thomas Cook would now find himself—his successors *do* find themselves—in a world preoccupied with "strategies", "targets" and measurable "outcomes", in which the educative purposes of tourism have been submerged within a "tourist industry", obsessed with national "image" and national wealth creation. The governments with whom he would deal would have specific "policies" on tourism, and would dictate to him the conditions under which he might arrange his clients' travel and accommodation. Most puzzlingly of all, he would find that no longer was one firm strongly identified

10 Piers Brendon, *Thomas Cook: 150 Years of Popular Tourism*, 1991, p. 6

11 *Cook's Excursionist*, May 1865

with one product or one service. He would find insurance companies that were also travel agents, travel agents that were owned by airlines, airline bosses that owned chains of record stores. He would find himself in a world where reaction to the *brand name* was more important than the products and services the name conveyed.

Nothing points up the contrast between the older style of management and modern managerialism more clearly than those modern managerial processes associated with *branding*. Once Shipham's Paste or Cherry Blossom Boot Polish or Timothy White's established themselves over time by the distinctiveness and quality of their products and services. That was how they "got their name". Now the name, or "brand", can be established quite independently of the customers' direct experience:

> Stephen Marks is making a fortune out of the f-word. Not the expletive, but "fcuk"—a clever and coincidental trademark and anagram. He has plastered the country with the nudge-nudge four letter logo on adverts as controversial, and publicity-generating, as Benetton in its heyday. The logo is a masterpiece of branding which has helped transform the 25-year-old French Connection from just another shop to an international name.
>
> The fcuk brand was dreamed up in-house. The company used to send faxes back and forth between its London and Hong Kong offices using the abbreviations FCUK and FCHK. "There was no thought of it being rude," insists Mr Marks, but advertising executive Trevor Beattie picked up on the abbreviation and came up with the "fcuk fashion" slogan.
>
> "I thought it was bloody marvellous," said Mr Marks. "We didn't even have an advertising budget at the time, but within four weeks we had the posters up and the rest is history."[11]

11 *The Independent*, 21 February 2001

Modern managerialists believe that a *brand*, once created and established, can be used to sell any kind of product. Whereas we might once have blenched at the thought of Reckitt's sausages, or Palethorpe's dyes, we are now persuaded to accept that a good brand name can be attached to anything.

Managerialists also believe, more damagingly, that any *cultural* body, any service or any voluntary activity, from political affiliation to fellwalking, can be "branded" and, if necessary, "re-branded" at will. Thus, to take a few examples at random, at the millennium the Tate Gallery was chopped in half like a garden worm, the resultant halves taking rebranded life as "Tate Britain" and "Tate Modern" respectively. Shortly afterwards the services of the Post Office were expensively rebranded as "Consignia"— though without any noticeable alteration in service. Then the Director of the Royal Shakespeare Company announced in May 2001 that his company was going to discontinue its previous policy of just presenting Shakespeare's plays, and instead develop a global brand of "RSC service". Most depressing of all, the government continued its policy of rebranding the whole of British culture as an *industry*, and an example from those same "cultural industries" will illustrate our contention that in the real cultural world the "rebranding" which invariably accompanies a managerial "relaunch" is the embrace of the vampire, a simulacrum of concern which drains the victim of life blood.

It is of course natural for a government to want to inform itself about the country which it governs. So, during the late nineteenth and early twentieth centuries, governments took careful note of the impressive economic growth of the British theatre. The *Theatres Report 1892* for example reported that there were no fewer than 1,300 licensed places of amusement in England alone, that the British theatre regularly employed more than 350,000 people and could be capitalised at more than £6,000,000.

Such reports contained factual information likely to be useful when matters of public legislation were being considered. By contrast, when in January 2000 The Arts Council of England commissioned a report on the "development" of what had once been called the provincial reps,[12] but which had now been rebranded as the English Regional Producing Theatres, it had a quite different intention.

The management consultants proceeded along familiar lines. The basic "fact" was that the ERPTs were, according to some calculations, losing audiences. They must therefore be in need of more management, new industrial "targets" and general rebranding. So, after talking to a number of arts bureaucrats the report's authors handed down nine industrial "targets" for the ERPTs which (it unblushingly assured us) were in accord with the Department of Culture, Media and Sport's "four main themes" and in line with *the government's central agenda*. First (and somewhat to the relief of theatregoers, who had feared that the national drama would not get a mention at all) the report conceded that the ERPTs should deliver "a national programme of quality live theatre"—although they did not spell out what sort of a programme this would be if theatre programmes really were aligned with the government's "central agenda".[13] The other targets in the rebranding process were even more problematic:

- Support a breadth and depth of programme in the regions
- Encourage new writing for the theatre and the wider creative industries

12. Peter Boyden Associates, *A Report for the Arts Council of England on the Roles and Functions of the English Regional Producing Theatres*, May 2000

13 Part of the government's central agenda is a desire to turn Britain into a multi-*cultural* state. This presumably means that British producing theatres would have to give equal weight to the performing arts of every culture. The sum is not easy to do, but we calculate that this means that on average each regional theatre will perform a play by William Shakespeare once every 2,144 years.

• Develop and nurture creative talent (including actors, directors, designers, musicians) for the theatre, film and television ecology
• Maintain and train the craft skill base for English theatre
• Support development at the small and middle scales
• Provide a potential focus for the celebration of local communities
• Deliver a wide range of theatre-related education and community programmes in collaboration with other service providers
• Deliver measurable local, regional and national economic benefits

It was immediately apparent that most of these targets could be achieved *without producing plays at all.* Indeed they would be *better* achieved if the HRPTs variously operated as churches, dance schools, music colleges, training units, internet cafés, craft centres, employment agencies, citizens' advice bureaux, social service teams or department stores— and if the HRPTs made the production of plays an occasional indulgence.

So why do professionals put up with it? Why do actors— and, come to that, teachers, social workers, doctors, priests, *all* professionals—not put a stop to the abstract dictates of modern managerialism? The advantages of being a top-flight modern manager—the adulation of politicians, massive salary, a "golden handshake" when your nostrums fail and you are forced out of your sinecure—are plain enough, but why do so many people lower down the pecking order, and in so many different realms, choose to behave as if there is no plausible alternative to being a state-managed zombie?

For example, when the government announced plans for a new "e-university" venture—"Just as other industries and services have restructured, so higher education can use global alliances to secure new forms of diversity with excellence for an expanded student population"[14]—why did university dons not simply laugh them out of court? Why did they not unite in protest against the way in which "excellence"—the very quality that universities exist to promote, and about which they supposedly know so much—was being appropriated and used as political ballast in the launch of a specious government policy?

The reason for such pusillanimous behaviour must partly be—to quote a well-worn adage—that it is unwise to bite the hand that feeds you. As the state has now extended its tentacles of licensing and control into almost every part of British life, virtually all negotiation over investment and funding—whether it be of universities, housing, hospitals, transport, social services, charities, schools or theatres—is now controlled by state bureaucrats. Such negotiation is not now pursued in well-established professional terms but in the language of modern managerialism; as industrial "investment" in "Great Britain Plc". Teachers no longer pursue the ideal of education for its own sake, but instead "deliver" measurable state "outcomes". The director of a provincial theatre no longer seeks to please a local audience, but to "deliver" a politically-sanitised programme of events. Whereas professionals once acted according to their own professional codes, they now act in accordance with state "targets" and "outcomes". In many realms the British worker is no longer a craftsman or a professional, but has been forced into acting as a state-controlled industrial automaton.

The entrapment is thoroughly enforced. As we have already shown, jobs of every kind are now advertised in the same abstract managerial terms. In their applications academics, teachers, architects, policemen, social workers and arts administrators are expected to enthuse about their willingness to "deliver" the quantitative "targets" which managerialism currently dictates. At interview applicants are expected further to demonstrate their allegiance to current managerial orthodoxy. Following their appointment their "performance" is regularly "assessed" by the controlling watchdogs according to the same managerial criteria. Finally, when they are ready to move on to another post it is their adherence to the managerial code which forms the substance of their official reference, rather than the individual qualities which may have made them good or bad practitioners. This means that our education system, for instance, is, in Sir Christopher Ball's words, "governed neither by principles nor by professional judgement, but by a complex interplay of funding régimes."[15] Workers of all kinds are thus continuously coerced into behaviour which may well run counter to their best professional instincts.

All this comes at a high price. Toeing the managerial line, and quieting the professional conscience, is for many people a stressful business. A 2001 survey pointed out that not just British academics but public sector workers generally were considerably less satisfied with their daily work than they had been ten years previously.[16] Occasionally the conspiracy of silence is broken, as when the Chief Inspector of Britain's prisons warned in a valedictory lecture in 2001 that the "cult of managerialism" was threatening the destruction of the prison system:

> When I asked the governor what was the aim of Parkhurst, he said it was to save £500,000 this year in the form of efficiency savings. I said that was not what I meant. I meant "Why should a prisoner be sent to Parkhurst and for what treatment?"
>
> He told me that this was the direction he had got from his line manager, and all his energies were devoted to identifying such savings which, inevitably, would be at the expense of the régime for prisoners.[17]

15 *The Guardian*, 19 June 2001

16 The study was by Professor Andrew Oswald and Dr Jonathan Gardner of Warwick University, reported in *The Guardian*, 22 March 2001

17 Sir David Ramsbothan, Public Lecture, 19 June 2001

In general however the imposition of managerialism is received with sullen acquiescence, in the belief that this is the only kind of behaviour, and language, which "they" understand. But such passivity quickly rots the professional fabric. Soon we start to observe those who should know better talking and acting like committed managerialists. Here for example is the Chief Executive of the Higher Education Funding Council for England, no less, assuring us that the quality of university research *can be measured by a simple mathematical formula devised by management consultants*. He tells us that in the year 2000 the HEFCE commissioned a review of research in British universities which concluded that "the research produced by academics in this country is among the best in the world. The number of times the work of UK researchers is read and used by other academics ('citations') per million pounds spent is the highest worldwide."[18] So the quality of universities can be measured by formula, just like sales in a department store. "Excellence" in research is a matter of first counting up the number of times British academics' names are mentioned in learned works, and then dividing the amount the British government spends on university research by that number. Of course, by this formula research "excellence" can be quantitatively increased, either by British researchers being encouraged to publish nonsense, thus gaining regular mentions as their work is demolished,[19] or by cutting government research monies even further, so that the number of "citations per million pounds spent" goes up.

If they are used frequently enough, the mechanical

18 Brian Fender, in a letter to *The Times*, 4 May 2001

19 We can easily demonstrate the fallacy in Mr Fender's argument by adding three citations to his personal count:: (a) Mr Fender does not have a clue about research excellence, (b) Mr Fender thinks like a pocket calculator, and (c) Mr Fender couldn't recognise real research even with his granny's glasses on. That such citations, even in a publication of the highest academic quality, merely add to a numerical total, and not to a qualitative appraisal, should be obvious even to the most compliant of managerial zombies.

abstractions of managerialism do not merely distort, but actually come to *replace* the evidence of the senses within the managerial world. This was vividly illustrated during the epidemic of foot-and-mouth disease which broke out in Britain during the Spring of 2001. 80,000 animal carcasses lay rotting in the countryside waiting to be burnt: all but one per cent of country footpaths within the infected areas were closed to the public. The former Bishop of Durham described the situation in these terms:

> Agri-business in the marketing of meat has evolved complex feeding practices and distribution systems which enable negligence on the part of a single operator to let loose a plague of apparently continental proportions. The slaughter of animals and the paralysis of the countryside which has followed are deeply shocking and cause depression and misery for many of our neighbours and fellow citizens.[20]

A few days before the Right Reverend David Jenkins's words, the then Culture Minister, Chris Smith, had been televised standing in front of an empty Cumbrian landscape. He was of course there to speak as spokesperson for the "Tourism Industry", which had as one of its major targets the achievement of an annual turnover of £12.5 billion—in part through attracting foreign visitors to roam the British countryside. Ignoring the roped-off footpaths, macintosh flapping like Merlin's cloak, jaw jutting against the wind and rain, eyes fixed upon the television cameras, the Minister offered this memorable incantation: "The British countryside," he averred, "is open for business as usual."

Mr Smith was not using those words with an intention to deceive. It would be nearer the truth to say that the language was using *him*, rendering him impervious to the fact that what he was doing and saying was contrary to the evidence of his senses. For the answer to the question why

20 Letter to *The Times*, 3 April 2001

modern managers behave as they do lies for the most part in the slippery and corrosive jargon which they use. It is to managerial language that we now turn our attention.

3

The Language of
Modern Management

Managerialism's drive to colonise, to extend its rule over all aspects and all areas of public life is fuelled by a relentless use of its own mechanistic language. The insistent linguistic modes of the managerial bureaucracies drive out all others. Under the guise of high seriousness, their own utilitarian language forms are imposed upon other ways of life, reducing their variety into managerialism's own uniformity. So symphony concerts, football matches, television soaps, volumes of poetry, pop festivals and art exhibitions are all called "products" that have to be "marketed", "delivered" or "rolled out". Once the health service had patients, education dealt with students and parents, the churches their believers, theatres their audiences, railways their travellers. Now all are "clients" or "consumers" of "services", because in abstract *management* terms their similarities seem to outweigh the enormous differences between real individuals and situations. If you are a client, then you are allotted statutory "rights", rather than having the power to enter into a personal agreement of your own choosing (and the swelling blame-culture that is driving people to seek redress and compensation demonstrates just one effect of accepting the new terminology). Change the accepted language, change the social structures and you change how people think and behave, even what they become.

Once you accept the language and hence the values of the market (enterprise, efficiency, growth, ambition, success) it transforms the world by changing the way that you see it. It is a commonplace nowadays to say that respect for the "community", for the public sector, for notions of caring, for professionally trained teachers, nurses and social workers has been eroded. The very notion of public service is unfashionable; now Whitehall prefers the term "social entrepreneurs" and everything must be a commercial "public-private partnership"—air traffic control, the National Theatre, prisons, the London underground, university research. The icons whom we are encouraged to worship are the rich: the go-getting entrepreneur, the dynamic manager, the famous sportsman, the wealthy movie star. People's aspirations are centred on the National Lottery and TV shows like *Who Wants to be a Millionaire?* Browsing through bookshops suggests that the desire for personal self-improvement (racks of magazines on slimming, fashion, homes and gardens) has now blended seamlessly with aggressive management guides, so that *How to Sell Yourself* and *Dress For Success* sit alongside *Power! How to Get It, How to Use It, Winning Through Intimidation, Predatory Marketing*. The underlying implication is that there are certain straightforward strategies—personal or corporate—that make success easier for you to attain. For those with limited reading skills, the authors boil books down to *The Fifteen Minute Money Manager* or *The Seven Habits of Highly Effective People*. The recommended book list from the Harvard Business School available on the internet shows the overwhelming popularity of certain keywords: "competing" and "competitive" are the most frequently repeated, followed by "winning", "capturing", "mastering", "maximising", "delivering", "leading". The overall impression is that individual success is all that matters.

So, generally unquestioned and with the connivance of government, managerial language seeps into every part of our lives, over-simplifying that which was enjoyably complex, and turning that which was warm and human into something cold and mechanical. We don't try to solve problems, we "address" them. We no longer have conversations with our friends and acquaintance, we "network". We no longer discuss an idea, we "lunch" it, like a business prospect. Things no longer "please" or "hurt" us—they "impact upon" us, like office franking machines. Our legitimate worries are now "stakeholder concerns", and our illegitimate worries symptoms of managerial malfunction, or "stress". We no longer correct our mistakes, we "revisit the data". Helping our families is "human resource management": bringing up our children is "parenting", while cooking them a meal is now "food technology".

It scarcely matters that these robotic terms are so often at odds with reality. We are so used to them that we utter them unthinkingly—we speak without irony of the "speed of change" as our rail systems collapse and our cities choke with traffic—because for so many people management language *is* now reality. People no longer feel instinctively that this mode of speech is out of place in home, school or church, and its habitual use makes us oblivious to its brutalities, and blind to the real human experience which it masks and distorts. A considerable number of British people have forgotten that, even a quarter of a century ago, it would have been thought manifest nonsense to say that the complexity and richness of the arts could be characterised as an "industry", that cathedrals must have managerial "mission statements", or that universities and hospitals should compete, like football clubs, for places in national "League Tables". It is not easy to say how our lives and thinking might be purged of the sticky taint of managerial language, but we can at least be aware of some of its worst manifestations. Although they are clearly interrelated, we can distinguish four chief modes in which management-speak operates, each with its own aim, style and envisaged audience.

First, there is the language of glossy public relations, where image and "presentation" are more important than information. This is the bland, banal language of the management consultant and the political spin-doctor. It is typically used to disguise the unpalatable—closures, redundancy, inconvenience, disaster—in saccharine terms that can hardly be demonstrated as either true or false. When the National Trust carried out a cost-cutting exercise that recommended job losses and the compulsory relocation of many staff, the director general presented the decisions in these terms: "The review will be able to provide us with the management structure we need to protect and nurture many good and successful things about the trust while moving forward to meet the challenges of the future."[1] Approving words (*protect, nurture, good, successful, challenge*) are piled together without actually saying anything.

We have become accustomed, even desensitised, to the way in which painful human realities are thus converted into impersonal deadness. The conventional excuses (like "the wrong kind of snow") have become so threadbare that they are now treated as black jokes: "we are having to downsize" (sack staff), "a negative patient outcome" (he died), "re-engineering the company" (trying to avoid bankruptcy). When the disaster is undisguisable, we are unctuously assured that "lessons have been learned" and that "robust action" will be taken in the future. When the accustomed definition of a term proves awkward—as when the numbers of "unemployed" seem to be rising, or there is a politically awkward increase in the numbers of those living in "poverty"—the definition may simply be changed to make the figures look better. At the most extreme, words can be redefined, Humpty Dumpty

1 Fiona Reynolds, reported in *The Guardian*, 28 March 2001

fashion, to convey whatever the writer chooses. For example, the screenwriter James Schamus has been quoted as saying that "Notions of authorship have been blown wide open. The author is really the person who owns the activity, who is paying the artists for their time while they are doing the work—that's the author."[2] So in his resolutely managerial definition, the "author" becomes the one with the money who pays the person who actually does the writing.

Government managers have proved adroit at adapting from business this blurring of the common language in a concern for "image". To be successful modern government policies and image have to be expressed in glowing terms that are memorable but deliberately imprecise, seemingly benign in character but planned to offend as few people as possible. Governments have learned from business that their political objectives, their "mission statements", need to sound warm and all-inclusive, but to be fuzzily expressed, with acceptable but blurred "targets". It is for example no longer expedient to have a clear "mission to pacify Ireland", but quite acceptable to say that you intend resolutely to "pursue the peace process".

How government actions are *perceived* thus becomes more important than the actual results of those actions. And it becomes an important step in the achievement of national health policy to appoint a "Director of Communications" in the government-funded *Commission for Health Improvement* (April 2000) with the following job-description:

> A senior communications professional with top level exposure to the complexities of the health scene, you will position us as the pre-eminent force for standards in health care. Your audiences will include a vast range of stakeholders, requiring both astute proactive planning and rapid reaction to complex issues.

2 Quoted in John Seabrook, *Nobrow,* 2000, p. 72

Implicit in this is the spin doctor's cardinal belief, that an organisation like the National Health Service does not become "pre-eminent" because of the way it does its job, the way it actually cares for the sick, but because of the way it is represented—that is, "positioned"—in the media, and hence the way it is perceived by the population at large—or, as the jargon describes them, the "stakeholders" in "the health scene".

A second language mode operates not by gloss but by piling up what seem incontrovertible "facts" and figures, in the conviction that these can be straightforwardly described because language simply reflects the "reality" under discussion. There seems no real awareness that the chosen language itself might shape the facts, or that facts are governed by their selection and interpretation. Strangely, the more that government and opposition speakers pour out conflicting facts and figures, the harder it becomes to make any sense of them. In 1999 an academic conference with the portentous title "A New Cultural Map" and aiming to define a "Research agenda for the Twenty First Century", no less, was held in the north of England.[3] One of the papers presented at it began like this: "There is no escaping from the fact that there is a need for good, hard, objective facts as the basis for cultural industries knowledge."[4] The speaker did not say whether this inescapable need was itself a "good hard objective fact", or a soft and subjective one, of the type we were being urged to leave behind. And it would have been pointless to put the question, for the proselytisers for the "cultural industries" believe, like Gradgrind in Dickens's *Hard Times*, that the necessary facts are all of one simple kind. For them modern "facts" are the cause and justification of every managerial process, of all cultural policy-making and of all

3 *A New Cultural Map: A Research Agenda for the Twenty First Century*: Proceedings of a conference held at Bretton Hall, University of Leeds, 19 July 1999, Bretton Hall, 2000

4 Sara Selwood, "Where is Research Going?" *A New Cultural Map*, p. 47

political action which follows upon it. Naturally, they were the basis for the government's *Annual Report 2000*. As the Prime Minister, adopting his own distinctive command of metaphorical language, proudly announced in his introduction:

> These are the facts. People can make their own judgement on them. But my assessment is that most of the key measures are going in the right direction. And for those which are not we are putting plans in place to turn them round . . . .[5]

It would appear that "facts" exist to serve the purposes of modern government managers, and if they do not point "in the right direction", they can be readily turned around. To qualify as a meaningful managerial tool, a modern "fact" must be promulgated and sanctified by government statisticians.

Writers and speakers in this mode concentrate on the measurable and the quantitative, with a balancing fear of "values" or "quality". A managerial "fact" is not just any piece of verifiable information. That Elgar composed the *Enigma* variations, that Shakespeare wrote *The Tempest* and that Constable painted *The Hay Wain* are facts, as is the joy that these works have brought to so many people a fact. But people's responses and judgements are not facts as modern managers and politicians understand them. Modern "facts" have to be quantitative, preferably couched in purely economic terms and must aim to reduce people to *things*—messy, unquantifiable life must be boiled down to equations. We see this in the Policy Studies Institute's infamous 1988 inquiry actually called *The Economic Importance of the Arts in Britain*. Its avowed aims were to uncover

> the value of the arts as a people magnet and the exploitation of the customer effect in regional eco-

5 Rt Hon. Tony Blair MP, Introduction to Government Annual Report, 2000

nomic development; the perceived value of cultural amenities as a business asset, a font of creativity and a valued amenity for the resident population; the role of the arts as a perceived amenity for tourism growth; and the cost-effective contribution of the arts as a means of cutting the unemployment count. (p. 8)

The authors, in the course of 221 closely printed pages, uncover such hard modern "facts" as "the arts formed a significant economic sector in their own right, with a turnover of £10 billion" (p. 61), "Cultural amenities were never an overriding consideration in the thinking of mover firms, but they could be an important complementary factor, reinforcing a predisposition to locate in a particular place" (p. 145) and "In an inner-city context, arts organisations of various different types can provide the social nodes around which future prospects can cohere" (p. 158). In such a world the quality of music, drama, art provided is of no inherent significance. The arts exist simply as economic goods, reinforcers of commercial predispositions or social nodes.

Our culture, our education systems, even our religions are now evaluated in tables of quantitative "facts". Thus the *Alpha* evangelical movement gains its significance primarily from the fact that it claims to have more than a million followers. Primary education, it is said, is being "reformed" because there is an annual percentage increase in youngsters' scores in state reading tests (without any consideration of what they *choose* to read). The works of younger British artists are claimed to be "world class" because of the large attendances at the London Tate galleries. At every level modern management apparently needs "facts", both to set it in motion, and to give it a destination, an easily recognised "outcome". Thus the authors were hardly surprised to hear a suggestion, at a serious discussion of counselling for the bereaved, that this operation could be improved by a simple quantitative adjustment—if the *average number of visits made by counsellors immediately after bereavement* were raised from two to three.

In this way the government forces us to consider the *quality* of our experiences only in terms of quantified managerial "objectives". Although looking after our health properly does involve some obviously quantifiable matters (are the right medicines available?) it is also a qualitative concern (do we trust the doctor?) In spite of this, modern management practice makes us focus upon purely quantitative matters. So if the waiting lists for hospital treatment come down, it will be suggested that this is proof that the *quality* of health service care is improving. The imposition of quantitative targets in areas where quality is the major consideration even extends to the management of personal relationships—as a recent advertisement for a new managerial post with the "Nottinghamshire Rural Community Council" indicates:

BEFRIENDING CO-ORDINATOR IN EAST BASSETLAW

The East Bassetlaw Befriending Scheme is a new partnership initiative which is also supported by Nottinghamshire County Council. The project aims to establish a volunteer befriending network throughout the villages of East Bassetlaw, offering friendship and support to isolated housebound residents.

The co-ordinator will be responsible for the running of the scheme, including the recruitment and training of volunteers and liaison with statutory and voluntary organisations.[6]

The Befriending Coordinator is to be set clear quantitative targets; he or she must liaise with other bureaucrats, and train volunteers to make a number of unsolicited offers of friendship to the targeted country dwellers. Whether any of these offers are taken up, and whether the isolated

6 *Nottingham Guardian Journal*, 4 December 1999

country folk enjoy the companionship of their newly-trained state friends are not prime concerns of the Befriending Co-ordinator. But this is unlikely to stop the authorities, once the quantitative targets have been achieved, from saying that the general level of friendliness has been raised, and that the quality of life in East Bassetlaw has been improved. Managerial target-setting of this kind almost always involves some sleight of hand with language, often (as in the foregoing example) falsely suggesting that matters of quality can be judged by reading off quantitative data. "Health care", "befriending" and "caring" all suffer in this way.

A third mode operates by translating everyday ideas into impressive-sounding managerial terminology, frequently splattered by acronyms. We are plunged into the world of "synergistic realignment", of "knowledge optimisation initiatives", of "strategic corporate criteria", and of "integration tools to leverage the utility"—whatever any of that might mean. Martin Sorrell, the business strategist known to *Sun* readers as "Mr £35 million", has said that he does not like the term "advertising agency", because "I prefer to use the term 'marketing communication services provider'."[7] His preference is a judgement on him. Industries and government present their objectives (or "targets") and policies (or "processes") in inscrutable and inhuman jargon to assure the general public that something valuable is going on, but in areas that are beyond the reach of any lay scrutiny. The terminology itself sounds impressively analytical, but in practice refers at best only to an idea (or attitude) held by the writer, and not to anything within the reader's experience. The terms are bolted tightly together, implying that there is a causal relationship between them, but, as in this example, they are usually related only by syntax and not by sense:

7 *The Guardian*, 23 August 1999

The establishment of minimum constraints for an optimisation of free growth combining elements of user-design for both the individual and the community, forms the basis of this project. The basic order devised is intended to establish a democratic interchange between human and technological factors. The order devised will stimulate multiplicity, multiformity, micro and macro relations: all expressed through logically derived dimensional and functional modules themselves articulated by a series of guiding lines.[8]

One variant of such essentially manipulative language is to present "arguments" in a form ensuring that any discussion can only be carried on within managerial premises. There is a bland assumption of values, aims and methods that many might not wish to support. So apparently unarguable statements are shaped by decisions already made and out of others' hands: "within current spending limits we have to . . ."; "of the two choices, it is clearly preferable to . . ."; "if we are to raise our position in the research league, then . . .". This common kind of "if . . . then" reasoning can be exemplified by this passage from a management website:

> If we accept the premise that knowledge management is concerned with the entire process of discovery and creation of knowledge, dissemination of knowledge, and the utilization of knowledge then we are strongly driven to accept that knowledge management is much more than a "technology thing" and that elements of it exist in each of our jobs.

Much virtue in an "if".

So it is that management experts will describe managerial processes in terms such as these:

> We need concepts and processes which give integrated approaches for dealing with multiple stakeholders on

---

8 Example offered by Kingsley Amis, *The King's English*, 1997, p. 12

multiple issues. For each major strategic issue we must think through the effects on a number of stakeholders, and therefore, we need processes which help take into account the concerns of many groups. For each major stakeholder, those managers responsible for that stakeholder relationship must identify the strategic issues that affect that stakeholder and must understand how to formulate, implement and monitor strategies for dealing with that stakeholder group. . . integrative metaphors are necessary which take into account the tried and true wisdom of "Customer service", "Employee participation", "Return to owners", etc. However these metaphors or organisational values must seek to integrate a number of stakeholder concerns.[9]

What this seems to be saying is that managers need to think and act in ways which take everybody's interests into account. By rolling together their variety into the banal term "stakeholder", this useful, if commonplace, idea is simultaneously made less precise and grotesquely aggrandised by the jargon used.

The pretentiousness of managerial language often has this curiously displacing effect of distracting the reader from what is really happening.[10] And at times it seems to cast doubt not just upon the wisdom of anyone having done what seems to be described, but also upon whether anything is really happening at all. So when we read that the Board of Marks and Spencers was determinedly going to "focus on strategic decisions"[11] we immediately assumed that the board was floundering and no longer knew what to do. Likewise when, following a report by leading management consultants, the Kent Police announced in the same year that they were now following "criminal

9 R. Edward Freeman, *Strategic Management: A Stakeholder Approach*, 1984, p. 24

10 In 2001 a manual was issued to bus drivers in Manchester on the effective management of their vehicles. It contained 183 "performance criteria" but did not mention the word "bus" once.

11 *Daily Mail*, 11 July 2000

incapacitation strategies", our faith in their ability to catch real criminals was immediately diminished. The adoption of high-flown managerial language—as when we are told that damaging closures are necessary for the "implement-ation of strategy", or swingeing price rises are inevitable for the "maintenance of trading position"—nearly always sounds like bluster, offered instead of a real excuse.

This is the mode particularly favoured by academics driven by a desire to establish what is still sometimes called the "science of management". Anxious to demonstrate that this is a "real" specialism, with its own specialist jargon, difficult for the uninitiated, they are still eager to import impressive terminology and concepts from other subject areas.

> In postmodernism, management is withered into vestigial form. Management is merely a transparent image, an arbitrary construct on free-flowing commod-ification.
>
> That is, it is an elusive if reified, meaningless sense-making device in a world that is impervious to control by (sensible) agents. Management is technology, the computer matrix a human product with a life of its own.[12]

Is deliberately riddling prose like this susceptible to para-phrase? Can management be both "image" and "techno-logy"? Does "meaningless sense-making" itself make any sense? Our reading repeatedly brings us up against prose that is bafflingly obscure, and yet apparently full of self-importance.

> The pejorative divisions that have characterised the development of organisational interpretation can be understood as redescribing and extending this separation of theory and practice. However, those very separations may also be read as oppositional commodifications that

---

12 Robert P. Gephart Jr, in Boje *et al.*, *Postmodern Management and Organisation Theory*, 1996, p. 41

expose complementary struggles for authority and privilege in bureaucratized workplaces within both academic and managerial work. Accordingly, from a postmodern position which articulates embeddedness as well as separation, the division of organisation and organisational analysis becomes decentered and relocated into concern for organising as a human practice. Here organisation becomes metaphorised into a human practice that is everyday, ordinary and extra-ordinary, whilst the articulation becomes a process of reflexive participation in the tensions, transience and possibilities of order/disorder.[13]

This is an extract from a lengthy paper first delivered to a management conference, where it was not only listened to attentively, but—according to the author—produced meaningful questions.

At the other extreme from those who write only for fellow management academics are those who write for a populist market of credulous would-be-successful managers. This fourth and final mode comprises those cosy narratives and parables, those examples of homely wisdom, offered by management "experts" to their eager disciples. It is hard to understand the immense popularity (and huge sales) of these guides. According to the Dilbert cartoons, the typical popular management book simply contains "a bunch of obvious advice with quotes from famous dead people". The market was given its first major boost by the runaway success in 1982 of *In Search of Excellence* by Tom Peters and Robert Waterman, which sold more than a million copies in its first edition. By 1983 there was a point at which the top three in the *New York Times* best-seller lists were all management texts—Peters's book, Ken Blanchard's *One Minute Manager* and John Naisbitt's *Megatrends*. Four years later one of Peters's many sequels, *Thriving on Chaos*,

---

13 Paul Jeffcutt, "The Interpretation of Organisation Studies" in *Journal of Management Studies* , vol 31. The paper was first presented at the Eighth International Conference on Organisational Symbolism.

spent a total of sixty weeks in the *New York Times* lists, comfortably outselling every work of fiction published in that year. America has since remained the prime home of the best-selling managerial authors—20,000 managerial books are now published each year in the USA—but in Britain managerial gurus such as Charles Handy and John Harvey-Jones have also achieved best-seller status.

Whether the purchasers actually *read* the books they buy in such numbers is rather more doubtful. A 1999 survey by researchers in *The Management Training Partnership*, for instance, suggested that only one in five of management books purchased is read all the way through. The newest and most fashionable, presumably, are briefly put on the office shelf to impress other managers, or are rapidly skimmed through on the train or plane journey. And a close perusal of a number of them does not yield many clues as to why they should be read with any kind of close attention. Popular management texts, like so many of the discoveries they reveal, are items of passing fashion. They depend on the reputation of some guru, who makes ambitious claims to transform managerial practice through some almost magical cure or nostrum. *Re-engineering the Corporation*, by Mike Hammer and James Champy, was impressively described as "a manifesto for a business revolution". One analysis suggests that these guru-authors are "part of a management-fashion-setting community" and their impact is based less on any expert knowledge than on their use of appealing myths and symbols. They "act as organisational myth-makers or story tellers" and part of their success is because they deliberately set out to give legitimacy to the aspirations and status-claims of the managers who buy and read their books.[14]

These books mostly seem to be written in the sort of snappy journalese of tabloid newspapers, which does not

14 Timothy Clark and Graeme Salaman, "Telling Tales: management gurus' narratives and the construction of managerial identity", *Journal of Management Studies* 35:2, March 1998, pp. 137–61

merit any close scrutiny. An extract from Peters's first best-seller conveys the characteristic tone:

> There is good news from America. Good management practice today is not resident only in Japan. But, more important, the good news comes from treating people decently and asking them to shine, and from producing things that work. Scale efficiencies give way to small units with turned-on people. Precisely planned R & D efforts aimed at big bang products are replaced by armies of dedicated champions. A numbing focus on cost gives way to an enhancing focus on quality. Hier-archy and three-piece suits give way to first names, shirtsleeves, hoop-la and project-based flexibility.[15]

Complex questions, social, religious or economic, are thus reduced to catchy mantras, and to confident assertions of the obvious. The reader is assumed to have a limited attention span, but to be in urgent need of conversion to the managerial cause, and so is addressed like a backward child in a missionary school. Indeed, the image is more apt than it may at first appear, for management texts frequently resemble children's stories. A modern manage-ment book such as Twyman Towery's *Wisdom of Wolves: Nature's Way to Organisational Success* or the best-selling management success of 1999, *Who Moved My Cheese?* could both be read to youngsters as undemanding bedtime stories. And some popular management authors, such as Roger E. Allen, actually flaunt their nursery orientation, as in this extract from the curious *Winnie the Pooh on Management*:

> The stranger was thinking about the Forest where Winnie the Pooh and his friends lived. At first glance it seemed a far different world from our everyday one of mindboggling change, constant crises, confrontations, insecurity, stress and ephemeral mortality.

15 Tom Peters and Robert Waterman, *In Search of Excellence; Lessons from America's Best-Run Companies*, New York, 1994, p. 119

However, that is only the way it seemed. "Pooh's world is actually much like ours," the Stranger thought. What could be more stressful than to be caught in a Horrible Heffalump Trap? Imagine the insecurity of being down to your last pot of honey with no bee-tree in sight or the unsettling change of having Strange Animals, who are generally regarded as one of the Fiercer Animals, move into your neighbourhood.[16]

"The stranger" decides that the adventures of Pooh and his friends could therefore be used to "illustrate and emphasise managerial skills" to business people, and the reader is expected to be convinced that the complex practices of modern management, which on the one hand purport to belong to a competitive adult world, can nevertheless be usefully conveyed by a rehash of a well-worn piece of childhood whimsy.

Even when popular management books seem on the surface to be rather more adult, there is still the sense of the reader sitting at the author's feet, living adventures vicariously, with the associated emotions prepackaged and handed down to them. There is frequently a note of school-teacherly condescension, as in the familiar chummy tones of the British management author, Charles Handy:

I have no hesitation in saying what is, for me, the greatest painting in the world. It is the Resurrection by Piero della Francesca. It is still where it was painted more than 500 years ago, on the wall in the town hall of Borgo San Sepolcro, a small Umbrian town. We should be thankful that frescoes are so very difficult to move, because it remains a thrill to make the journey across the Italian hills to that small town, to walk into the room where Piero painted and to see before you what he did for his fellow citizens.

This has the customary omniscience of the modern guru—a writer who knows where the world's best art is to

16 Roger E Allen, *Winnie-the-Pooh on Management*, 1995, pp. 159–60

be found, who experiences a thrill on our behalf by going to look at it, and who kindly explains for us the artist's motives. Yet what is so obviously lacking, amongst much else, is any real willingness or desire actually to engage the reader. There is no attempt to appeal to the reader's experience, to suggest why this is, for Handy, the "greatest painting in the world". The whole passage is bolted together from the threadbare terms of a guidebook and conveys nothing truly felt. What did "that small town" actually look, feel, and smell like? How exactly did he "make the journey" across the Italian hills? What *sort* of "thrill" did he have, and at which point did he actually experience it? It conveys less than even the poorest novel—but that does not prevent Handy from drawing the most sweeping conclusions from his "experience":

> Everyone draws their own message from great art. For me the Resurrection carries a metaphorical meaning rather than a conventional religious one. I am free, goes that message, to break free from my past and to recreate myself. . . . It may be that I shall not see the full result of my efforts, but I should so strive that others may profit, even if it be after my death. This is the sort of immortality I can understand. It is a message that applies to all people, and to all businesses and institutions. The best is always yet to come if we can rise from our past.[17]

Yet the conclusion, for all its seeming air of homely profundity, is confused and almost meaningless. "If we can rise from our past", he grandly but somewhat obscurely informs us, "the best is always yet to come." The sentiment—whatever it may actually be—is considerably less profound than the "conventional" religious message of the Resurrection which Handy seeks to supplant. Handy's managerial homily is, at every level and for every purpose, incomparably less meaningful than the "conventional" Biblical story.

17 Charles Handy, *The Hungry Spirit*, 1997, p. 263

Management texts are full of such trite conclusions, usually drawn from badly-recounted and highly improbable "anecdotes". Here is an example drawn from another management book—from the beginning of a chapter unironically called "Culture and Management":

> An Israeli making a first visit to the United States visited an international trade fair in New York. The crowds leaving the fair were massive, and a policeman was stationed to signal that pedestrians could only make a right turn into the neighbouring streets. The crowds followed his instructions. The Israeli followed suit but afterwards confessed his astonishment: "In Israel there would always be a wise guy who would figure out that if a policeman told you to go right it's better to go left. America is much more disciplined." But while the Israeli sees evidence of discipline in the Americans' relationship with authority, a German or Frenchman might think pedestrian behaviour to be far more chaotic in the United States than at home.

The reactions of anyone who had read thus far will surely be that this is a very poorly realised picture of New York. Can we really believe that there, of all cities, crowds would pour directly out of an international trade fair directly on to the streets, without barriers being erected, and with a solitary "policeman" stopping them from turning left? The characters are equally poorly realised, adopting childishly simple national stereotypes. That said, it is something of a surprise to learn the sweeping conclusions drawn from such an improbable anecdote:

> Your cultural priorities determine your behaviour with other people and influence your attitudes towards other people in the organisations to which you belong. Specifically, they influence how you manage and expect to be managed, and how you communicate within the organisation.[18]

18 Richard Mead, *Cross-Cultural Management Communication*, 1990, p. 13

For the anecdote, such as it is, has in fact shown the opposite to be true The credulous Israeli (who comes, it seems, from an ill-disciplined culture) has *not* allowed his behaviour to be determined by his assumed "cultural priorities". He has, like the improbably created crowd of New York businessmen, meekly followed the single policeman's instructions. In any case the anecdote has told us nothing about the *organisations* to which these people belong, only that American, Israeli, German and French nationals allegedly behave in certain stereotyped ways.

It is only the language of tabloid journalism and management text-books which allows such horrors. No novelist, and come to that no historian or journalist—or even a children's story book writer—could get away with such a ridiculously improbable picture of life on the New York streets. But here all disbelief is suspended because it is a *management* book. And in such books people do not behave as you and I. They do not laugh and love, eat and drink, sleep and dream. Modern managerial language of the kinds discussed in this chapter has had all complexity, nuance and irony sucked from it, so that what remains is flat and non-problematic, often precluding any possibility of reasoned debate. Yet the gurus of modern management would of course prefer their dehumanising language to remain unexamined: it can hardly be accidental that the term "language" features so seldom in the indexes or contents lists of standard management texts. Whereas genuine disciplines are forever questioning how their language constitutes reality, there seems an astonishing lack of curiosity about this from management writers. When they do touch on the subject (nearly always preferring the mechanistic word "communication") it is virtually always as a branch of problem-solving: how the manager can communicate more efficiently with the work-force, or with folk from other cultures.

This can hardly be accidental. What can be said about management depends on the language at one's disposal. Those infected with the managerial virus would not wish their assumptions and doctrines to be discussed in any language but their own. Meanwhile, those outside the enchanted circle find themselves increasingly mired in managerial newspeak, as more and more academic texts, professional conferences and meetings in schools, hospitals, and social services adopt that same deadening managerial language to describe their purposes and functions. When, just before the 2001 election, Education Minister David Blunkett set out his "vision" for the future of British universities, he said that the government sought to "foster the transfer of knowledge held within universities to business". It was in truth hard to see any need for more fostering, as successive governments had effectively ensured that the language of management shaped what was regarded as useful knowledge. It is already a distinguishing characteristic of modern universities that *most* of their meaningful conversations are with businessmen.[19]

19 For instance, in response to Mr Blunkett's "vision", the Vice Chancellor of London's City University proudly wrote that "Our strategic aims—set last year—and our actions since, anticipated many of the Secretary of State's views. . . . The University—in accordance with its strategic aims—is much involved with public affairs in the metropolis. We participate actively in the London First business-led consortium to bolster London's economic and cultural successes."

4

Management as an Academic Subject

In Britain today far more students (one in seven of them) enroll on courses in business or management than in any other field of study. The numbers are still rising, though there is still some way to go before we catch up with the United States, where a quarter of all those entering graduate courses are studying management. Yet in spite of this overwhelming popularity, it is by no means certain that "management" has any validity as an academic discipline, still less as a self-contained university subject. There remains considerable confusion about what management-as-subject comprises, what education in it should aim to do, and what methods might achieve these ends. Schools of Management vary considerably in their approaches and in their subject matter, which change almost year by year. Whereas a student entering a university course in History or Physics, Philosophy or Medicine, will have at least some notion of what is involved, "Management", though highly fashionable, can apparently mean almost anything. Why this should be the case, and what the results have been, emerge from the way in which the supposed "subject" came to be.

Before the 1939–45 War, formal education for management hardly existed in Britain; there was virtually no demand for it from government, industry or the universities. When a special committee was set up in 1947 to consider whether there should be some national scheme of management education, their report began by frankly asserting that "there is no implication in this report that young men or women can be trained as managers in industry and commerce by following certain courses of study."[1] How is it, then, that such courses have spread rampantly through British higher education?

In retrospect, the influence of that 1947 report was significant in two ways. First, it established a pattern of fairly low-level certificates and diplomas grounded in technical colleges, which left those teaching them hungry for higher status and influence. Second, it assumed that there would be a wide variety of different courses, tailored to particular local situations. At this time "management" was thought of in Britain as no more than a convenient umbrella term without any suggestion that it defined some coherent subject. When the *Association of Teachers in Management* framed a symposium of papers on management studies in 1966, it drew on sixteen different subjects, and the editor said frankly that this was on the "cafeteria service" principle, so that those running courses could "try out anything which takes their fancy".[2] Accounting, Law, Sociology and Economics formed, he said, "only one part of a much wider field." This was, at least, honest and clear. Students who emerged from college with a grounding in accounting, law, personnel management or marketing would possess recognisable qualifications seen as appropriate for their particular situations and careers.

But the volume had another, less respectable, purpose. The Foreword makes clear that it was not disinterested, but the work of specialists with their own agenda, who wanted

1 Urwick Committee, *Education for Management—Management Subjects in Technical and Commercial Colleges*, HMSO, 1947, p. 4

2 Derek Pugh (ed.) *The Academic Teaching of Management*, Association of Teachers of Management, Occasional Paper 4, Oxford, p. 2.

to create and establish a new curriculum subject. They and others during the 'sixties helped to prompt the growing belief that Britain's poor industrial record was significantly attributable to "inadequate managerial performance" and that therefore economic growth would be aided by courses to improve managerial quality. Simultaneously they asserted that both in the business world and in higher education the climate was becoming "more sympathetic" to management education, increasingly accepting its "academic potential" to convey "universal" and transferable principles and techniques. With hindsight, it is surely clear that neither of these assumptions rested on any firm evidence. Was managerial performance a more significant reason for industrial weaknesses than, say, underinvestment, worldwide economic factors, government policy or outdated labour conditions? What evidence was there that universal managerial theories and practices actually existed and could be straightforwardly conveyed to students from different cultures?

Beneath the high-sounding rhetoric, what the members of the group wanted is clear. First, they wished to present themselves as members of a profession, which they attempted to do simply by asserting that it was so. Such claims have not been generally conceded, except in a limited way, up to the present, and more will be said of this later in the chapter. Second, they wanted to establish management as an academic subject in its own right. What was to be taught was seen as much less significant than the urgent need to "justify" the wider acceptance of the subject and to assert that it would have "academic respectability". Those involved, said the editor, had to ensure that proposals for management-as-subject were not seen as a soft option, and that remarks such as "A degree in Management—Huh! They'll be having one in paper-hanging next!" had no justification. To "accelerate the professionalization of management" and to give it "respectability", he went on, required "high standards for entry, a long and arduous course, a respectable failure rate (i.e. respectably high)". The aim was "that by the year 2,000 there would be no managers without formal training in the subject". It was frankly admitted at the time that—

> Management education is not a homogeneous "product", or even an easily identifiable group of "products". There exists a wide variety of possible types of course, differing in objectives, in form and in quality.[3]

More than twenty years after the ATM Symposium, an international volume again concluded that "there is little agreement on what subjects should constitute a management training or education course" and went on to list 43 disciplines or skills currently on offer to students.[4] In the nineteen-eighties it could be lamented that "the goal of an integrated, coherent and relevant 'science of management' seems, if anything, further away than it did in the halcyon 1950s," because of a continuing lack of connection between "the highly differentiated and specialised subfields of management education".[5]

However, the piecemeal nature of what passes for management education, candidly termed "fragmented adhocracy", still tends to be conveniently ignored by many of those in the business. Students may emerge from the first degrees on offer in business and management at British universities with virtually no common knowledge or experience. They may have been involved in computer science, European studies, law, marketing, accounting, human resources, economics, finance, operations management, or social administration. Syllabuses show that they may or may not have chosen courses in international

3 H. B. Rose *et al.*, *Management Education in the 1970s: Growth and Issues*, HMSO, 1970, p. 60
4 William Byrt (ed.), *Management Education: an International Survey*, 1989, pp. 213–14
5 Richard Whitley, "The fragmented state of management studies: reasons and consequences", *Journal of Management Studies*, 21:3 (1984) pp. 331–48

politics, contract law, dance and drama, the European Union, enterprise skills, research skills, software development, social issues or team building.

The reason for this incoherence is plain. At no stage did any agreed thinking emerge beyond vague generalities to suggest precisely what knowledge base the emerging "discipline" should have, what abilities it might inculcate in students or what methods were best designed to develop them. In the evolution of Management-as-subject, a number of quite different and only loosely associated pressure-groups, with varying degrees of "academic respectability", came together with the intention of claiming some wider (but undefined) disciplinary status. The agenda for this claim was struggled over by conflicting interests and groups, with only a tenuous connection between them and without any shared sense of overall strategy. The warnings of the 1947 Urwick Committee about avoiding the multiplication of courses[6] were simply ignored. Springing up in one university after another, the new "subject" defined itself in each as it went along, according to existing staffing, resources and expertise within the institution rather than being decided by any agreed overall principles. What happened can be seen as a continual series of adjustments and alliances according to circumstances, opportunities and a perceived market.

Uncertainty about the subject itself was mirrored by uncertainty about who was qualified to teach it. Rose's significant report of 1970 (already cited) suggested serious doubt whether the staffing of universities entering this field was adequate to provide appropriate courses: "Our general impression is of a widespread and serious scarcity of teachers possessing the combination of academic quality, business experience and personal characteristics needed by the effective management teacher." (p. 28) What

6 The second recommendation was about avoiding the proliferation of courses, noting that "so long as each professional institution requires its own syllabus in this field, this must create difficulties . . . ." (Urwick Report, p. 4)

sort of person might have been recognised as an "effective management teacher"? In the late nineteen-sixties, virtually none of the full-time university teachers had qualifications in management (unsurprisingly, since the subject had no real existence at the time). This meant that the "subject" evolved largely in terms of related but better established disciplines, taking on the traditional ways of thinking and acting found in economics and mathematics, sociology, law, social psychology and social anthropology. Numerically, the greatest number of those teaching management came from the behavioural sciences, then those qualified in mathematics and statistics, followed by economics, finance and accounting. In the early stages it was specialists in those subjects who were largely responsible for teaching and assessment, sometimes those who were unable to gain posts in mainstream disciplines. Their influence has continued to dominate by pulling the thinking within management education in the direction of their own specialisms and discourses to the exclusion of others. Two key questions were not answered then or since. First, when traditional subjects like Economics, Law or Statistics are offered, what—if anything—is the specific *management* element that separates the course from that offered to students in the mainstream subjects? Second, is academic training in subjects like these that *appear* to have some connection with management necessarily the best education for the actual task of managing?

The first entrepreneurial lecturers to claim ownership of this ambiguous field realised the importance of creating a distinct market for teachers like themselves, who would progressively be able to insist that university posts should go to those with academically certified qualifications in that area. In a similar way, as management sought to colonise other activities (terming them Cultural Industry, Leisure Industry, Hospitality Industry and so on: a process described elsewhere) courses sprang up to teach how to "manage" them, and their first graduates inevitably came to dominate appointments within those emerging fields. The existence of a pool of such specialists (originally a very small one) meant that there was a high degree of mutual dependence. Today, even within the supposed field, there is little evidence that those who teach it see management as an accepted discipline. One of the rare studies of management educators (though based on a small sample) concluded that few of those teaching management actually saw the subject as their first choice. One typical respondent said: "If I had been a good enough historian I would much have preferred to stay in History. I went into management schools because they were expanding and there were lots of jobs going... I don't see myself as a teacher of management, I don't think it is a discipline."[7]

Such dissatisfaction with most of what passes for management education has led a number of scholars, from quite different theoretical positions within the field, to unite in expressing grave concern about its ineffectiveness. They claim that there is too little attention to teaching students how to learn and think, and too much indoctrination and examining out-of-date business anecdotes. Indeed, some now argue that the attempts to establish management as a separate field have been misguided. Looking at a number of works of the nineteen-nineties makes clear that critics believe that "there is something seriously amiss", that there is widespread "disillusionment with traditional forms of management theory and practice", that "much of management education is irrelevant and some of the rest is naive", that it relies unquestioningly on "taken-for-granted assumptions" drawn from a "canon" of approved writers, sometimes bordering on "frank charlatanism". Authors point to "the lack of a clear disciplinary focus", to a knowledge base that "is

7 Ardha Danieli and Alan B. Thomas, "What about the Workers?: Studying the role of management educators and their orientations to management education", *Management Learning* 30 (4) 1999, pp. 440–71

fragmented and disputed," and to a concentration on specific skills that will become obsolete before they can be put into practice. Overall, we are told of "mounting evidence" that "a specialized management education does nothing or does harm."[8]

The many internal critics unite in suggesting that managers need an education radically different from the one traditionally offered. However, even if we welcome the late nineties' new emphasis on human and analytical skills, learning to learn, flexibility, concern for social and moral values, awareness of other cultures and behaviours, the capacity to see different perspectives and conceptions of truth and right, questions still have to be asked. First of all, if we wish students to develop these valuable abilities, would we send them to Business Schools in the first place? Would they not do better to study philosophy, history or literature, subjects which are already directed that way? Even at the utilitarian level, there is little evidence to suggest that a sound general education damages later managerial performance. Secondly, the abilities being detailed are surely not seen as applicable only to those studying management. A manager in a large car manufacturing firm has written that he sees the essential qualities for new recruits as including flexibility, self-reliance, capability with Information Technology, leadership and teamwork skills, an international focus and ability in problem solving. But as Business Schools rush to assure potential students that such "skills" (another dangerous term) are developed as "an integral part" of their courses,

8 Comments here and in the following paragraph are drawn from C. Grey and N. Mitev, "Management Education: a Polemic", *Management Learning* 26 (1) 1995, pp. 73–90; M. Alvesson and H. Willmott, *Critical Management Studies*, 1992; P. D. Anthony, *The Foundation of Management*, 1986; J. Kallinikos, "Mapping the Intellectual Terrain" in R. French and C. Grey (eds) *Rethinking Management Education*, 1996; A. B. Thomas and P. D. Anthony, "Can Management Education be Educational?", in French and Grey, 1996; A. Mutch, "Rethinking Undergraduate Business Education", *Management Learning* 28 (3) 1997, pp. 301–12. The case for a wholesale redesign of management education is given fuller treatment in Protherough's "Reconstructing the Study of Management" in David Golding and David Currie (eds) *Thinking about Management*, 2000, pp. 65–80.

are they suggesting that those like teachers, nurses, journalists, and social workers—for whom these abilities are equally important—could be simultaneously trained in their institutions? Is this part of the subject's colonising tendency to turn everything else into itself? The supreme irony is that Business Schools and Schools of Management so often reveal (or try to suppress) glaring weaknesses in their own management. Official reports repeatedly refer to their "problems of internal management and control", "concerns over teaching and learning standards". Compared with other subjects, they often admit difficulties in attracting high-calibre students, high drop-out rates and low proportions of higher degree students that actually complete.

The pervasive vagueness about what claims—if any— management has to be seen as a subject or discipline is inevitably related to a wider uncertainty about what it means in the world of work. Contemporary writers of texts on management seem to be agreed on the difficulty or impossibility of defining what management is or what managers do. "There is no straightforward answer to the question" (Christopher Grey), "there is no simple answer" (Rosemary Stewart), because the terms are "slippery", "tangled", or "questionable", and are "used in so many different ways". Many authors simply avoid trying to say what, if anything, the words mean for them. One recent book (published in 2000) questions the value of making "attempts to reach definitive or generalised conclusions about the nature of management".[9] Instead we are told defensively that "managers do a large number of different things" (Salaman), that these "defy description and analysis," that "remarkably little is known about the particular skills or competencies required by managers" (Barry) and that the role of management is "to integrate a complex set of

9 David Golding and David Currie (eds) *Thinking about Management: A Reflective Practice Appproach*, 2000

human and organizational variables" (Freedman). "Diversity makes it far from easy to generalise about what managers do, or indeed to make any coherent sense of management at all" (Sjostrand). Well, that's that, then.

When we are offered a definition, it is frequently couched in management-speak, turning a platitude into ideological jargon:

> We define management as the activities of social actors and their interventions into organized human processes, particularly actors with discrete formal statuses that provide the legitimate authority to direct and coordinate the behaviour of other social actors.[10]

If we turn to dictionaries or encyclopaedias the situation is no better. We find that their definitions are circular or question-begging: Management is "the action or manner of managing", says the *Shorter Oxford*, and a manager is "one who manages", or—in other sources—"a person who directs or manages an organization, industry or shop" (*Collins*), or more grandiloquently is "A term applied to employees who direct supervisory personnel to attain operational goals of an organisation or department as established by management" (*US Dictionary of Occupational Titles*). Such "definitions" could equally well apply to policemen on traffic duty, mothers with children or carers in old people's homes. Elsewhere we are hardly surprised or enlightened to be told by an encyclopaedia that "Industrial management is concerned with the management of manufacturing enterprises." One respected writer on management concludes: "Any definition of management must be right, because almost any definition must fit something so amorphous and shifting."[11]

This inability to define the nature of management surely undermines any claims for it to be considered a profession.

10 D. M. Bose, R. P. Gephart Jr, T. J. Thatchenkery (eds) *Postmodern Management and Organization Theory*, 1996
11 Robert Heller, *The Naked Manager for the Nineties*, 1995, p. 13

Books on medical training are clear about the doctor's role: to assess and diagnose, to treat, prescribe or refer, to monitor and so on. Solicitors are defined as those with knowledge of the law that enables them to advise clients, to draw up documents, to prepare cases for barristers. Doctors and solicitors may specialise in certain aspects of their work, but there is general agreement about what they are *for*, what it is they *do*. One can then go on to assess the relative effectiveness of the professional education offered in various universities. Our concern about management is that the defensiveness about its shifting and uncertain meanings simply reflects a much deeper uncertainty about function. One specialist in professional education has said that unless we can say what a profession *does* there is no possibility of "analysing its practice, training its practitioners or evaluating its performance".[12] Posing the question "What does the word professional mean in the context of managing?" Professor Mintzberg admits that it is plainly different from medicine or engineering; "formal education can hardly be considered a prerequisite to practising this so-called profession."[13] There is no certainty that an untrained manager will be less effective than a trained one, whereas there is a general assumption that training is essential for doctors and solicitors. The aims of medicine and the law and the ways of achieving them are largely agreed, and can be transferred from one situation to another, but—as we argue in chapter one—this is not true of management.

It should in honesty be said that the marks of professional status, once apparently clear, have become blurred in recent years by the rapid growth of managerialism. In the nineteen-sixties the position of the professions, laboriously built up, seemed distinct and secure. However, this was before a major political assault supported by free-

12 Geoffrey Squires, *Teaching as a Professional Discipline*, Brighton, 1999, p. 29
13 H. Mintzberg, *Mintzberg on Management*, New York, pp. 348–9

market economics, consumer dissatisfaction and radical theoretical critiques. It proved easy to attack the work of professionals by complaining that some were less effective than others, that they were sometimes inherently conservative, that they placed their own interests above those of their "clients". Well, of course. Could anyone living in the real world be surprised at such a comment on *any* group of working people? But the proposed remedy—increasing managerial and ideological control of the professions—is manifestly flawed, as we argue. The deliberate policy of moving managers into key positions in professional organisations and of persuading professionals to take on more and more managerial functions has simply muddied the concept of professionalism while doing nothing to strengthen management's claims to be seen as professional.

Such claims have come most strongly from the established business schools, offering the Master's degree in Business Administration, a qualification embodying American colonialism and the desire to reshape European higher education along American lines. In 1956 the Economic Planning Agency was persuaded to send over fifty European university teachers to the US to learn management subjects at American universities. Influential British businessmen were invited to attend courses at the Harvard Business School. Simultaneously, American academics such as Professor Harry Johnson of Chicago were helping to restructure the curriculum at institutions like the London School of Economics. It was the American example that inspired the creation of two new British business schools in London and Manchester and overwhelmingly influenced the later spread of courses throughout higher education. Now, to quote one glowing account, the MBA in Britain "has truly come of age; a flagship management development programme with some 12,000 students a year studying in Britain" providing specific training for many occupations, "even footballers". As well as the classic *generalist* MBA it is now indeed possible to take so-called *niche* courses in "football-related industries", "pop music management", "leadership skills", e-commerce, church, maritime, financial or oil and gas management. This massive expansion has been "breeding a new race of management technocrats, whose salaries are measured in telephone numbers and who can downsize a multinational in a matter of minutes."[14]

Under the modest heading "Pillars of the Economy", the web site of The Association of Business Schools asserts proudly that "Britain is a world leader in management education and training." Quite apart from what it calls "the explosion in demand" from home students, business schools attract more than 36,000 European Union and other overseas students annually to study in the UK. This unprecedented popularity is attributed to a growing desire for "study which combines academic rigour with practical relevance". Cynical academics suggest that the comparatively relaxed demands of "top-up" degrees and "while-you-work" qualifications in business may have more to do with it. However, management qualifications like the MBA, the web site assures the reader, are seen by students as "a passport to gaining new challenges and responsibilities in their careers and to achieving greater competence in the wide-ranging roles demanded of them by their employers". In view of all this hectic enthusiasm, it is surely surprising that, according to one recent newspaper survey, the top two hundred managers in Britain cannot summon up a single MBA between them.

The glossy advertisements for MBA courses contrast interestingly with the relatively sober invitations to apply for other advanced academic courses. They use the snappy language of public relations and are big on vague promises, suggesting that they can help you to "move your

14 *The Guardian*, 22 January 2000

career in any direction you choose" (Henley), "connect to the future" (Cambridge), bring you "accredited success" in "a world of opportunity" (Manchester Metropolitan), "developing global competence for a changing world" (Birmingham); they can "bring out the best in you" (Lancaster), help you "to achieve excellence" (Leeds), "make your mark in the new millennium" (North London), "achieve your management potential" (Kingston), increase your "earning potential" (Leicester), or even "change your life" (Thames Valley). Who could resist (assuming that they can afford the £20,000 for the full-time Cranfield programme, say)?

Which institution to choose? A 1997 survey by the Economic Intelligence Unit found that by far the commonest reason for choosing a course was "Reputation of School". Reputation is a slippery concept in a world where all the institutions realise how dependent they are on the image created. Shall it be "the best in your chosen field" (Lancaster), "in a class of its own, recognised and respected throughout the world" (Henley), "a nationally and internationally recognised centre of business learning" (Sheffield), "a first class international university" (London), "one of Britain's leading research universities" (Warwick), "one of the UK's leading centres for management education" (Nottingham), one with a "reputation for trailblazing research and academic excellence" (City), "a world ranking business school" (Manchester), "internationally accredited" (Leicester), "one of the UK's leading creative universities" (Goldsmiths) or simply "a friendly and flexible university" (North London)?

As they jostle for market share, they each advance claims that implicitly denigrate others, rather like car manufacturers: "our research faculty already has the best rating in the UK", "excellent teaching ratings", "the best value London MBA", "the premier distance learning MBA". They assure students that they can provide "the sharp edge of theory and practice" (whatever that means), "maximum flexibility in when and how you study", a course "tailored to your needs", "located in one of Europe's most idyllic cities" or "at the heart of one of the world's most exhilarating business centres, where the networking opportunities are unmatched". As a lecturer at the Judge Institute, Cambridge, remarks sardonically: "The attraction of most MBA courses seems tacitly to depend on the insecurities or egoistic ambitions of the students."[15]

Despite all the high-powered publicity, the educational value of this qualification is increasingly being questioned by those outside the magic circle, by employers and academics. "Can you name an expensive, over-supplied product whose suppliers and customers alike are deeply unsure about its value and specification? . . . It's the business school degree, the MBA, itself."[16] It claims to be a postgraduate degree, and yet large numbers of those gaining it have no first degree. Following Lord Dearing's report and the pressure for clearer definition of qualifications, there is increasing unease about calling the MBA a Masters degree at all. In addition, its value to the business careers of those so expensively educated has been questioned. According to Heller, more graduates from Harvard and similar institutions go into teaching within business schools and into consultancy than into the world of work—unsurprisingly, since MBA courses do not teach how to manage.[17]

The results of this unbridled growth in management-as-subject have proved damaging to higher education in Britain. "Business and management disciplines now dominate British universities as never before", writes Graham Wade[18] and this is not only true in terms of

---

15 Quoted *Rethinking Management Education*, p. 68

16 *The Naked Manager for the Nineties*, p. 306

17 *Ibid*, pp. 313, 324. The same pattern apparently applies in Britain, according to the 1999–2000 survey of the Association of MBAs. However, two critics point out that "No one MBA programme in the UK (and probably in the world) teaches 'managing' as a separate subject. There are no professors of 'managing' in the UK." (*The Observer*, 20 May 2001)   18 *The Guardian*, 18 January 2000

student numbers. As we were writing, the annual survey of top academic salaries in the UK revealed that top of the tree, well ahead of all vice-chancellors, was Professor John Quelch, then head of the London Business School, who earned—or, at least, got—£252,000 a year. Professor Quelch was happy to defend this gross difference from the pay of other academics. Inevitably his argument rested on "market forces" and "the need to compete". He repeated the free-market assertion that we must follow the American pattern, where salaries in business schools are higher than in the arts and sciences. "Salaries at the London school reflect its *Financial Times* ranking as the best business school in Europe."[19] This is just one example. As they have gained in status (and particularly in the ability to recruit profitable students from overseas) management specialists have progressively convinced their parent universities that they required enhanced salaries, low teaching and administrative loads, hefty travel grants and research support. If these were not forthcoming, or if the university demanded a slice of their consultancy fees, then professors threatened to go elsewhere and take their connections with them. This situation has been entertainingly but savagely described by Professor Nigel Piercy, who sees business school professors as an unproductive group who have to be subsidised by their colleagues. He divides them into four categories: cowboys ("who take all that they can get" and have their names on research papers without doing the work), quislings (who take the benefits but "yearn to be proper academics" in a real discipline), chameleons (torn between the rival attractions of academic work and independent consultancy), and question-marks (for whom there may still be some hope). He claims that most of these are "cheating" and "spreading poison", and his conclusion is: "We have given business school professors all the things they needed to achieve excellence and they have not delivered."[20] Robert Locke widens the complaint beyond such "dangerous pretensions" to higher salaries and extra earnings. He believes that business school staffs are so insulated from their universities that they show "indifference" towards colleagues outside the business school, and remain unaware of what is going on in their institutions.[21]

Nearly half a century ago in the United States William H. Whyte was pointing out some of the ways in which the swing towards business studies not only damaged recruitment for traditional disciplines but was also "subtly changing the climate of the whole campus."[22] As an example, he cited the "destructive influence" at the University of Pennsylvania of its business school, the well-regarded Wharton School of Finance and Commerce. As its business courses became more popular, so the climate in the university became increasingly non-intellectual and non-academic, discouraging interests in the theoretical sciences and the liberal arts. The growth and prestige of vocational courses was further bolstered by the grants and support provided by those commercial bodies that believed themselves to be somehow validated by the business school courses offered as preparation for them. Academics who would privately express horror at increasing materialism suddenly became supine when faced with the demands of grant-givers. More recently at Oxford, opposition to the development of the Business School and its new buildings was suddenly muted after a major donation from Mr Wafic Said, a Saudi businessman, which also resulted in the renaming of what is now the Said Business School. Hardly had work begun on its new buildings when the head of the school, John Kay, resigned, blaming the university's unwil-

20 Nigel Piercy, "In Search of Excellence among Business School Professors", *European Journal of Marketing*, 33 (7/8), 1999, pp. 698–706

21 Robert R. Locke, *The Collapse of the American Management Mystique*, Oxford, 1996, pp. 231–2

22 William H. Whyte, *Organization Man*, Penguin edn, 1956, p. 82

lingness to change. Specifically he claimed that it was impossible to attract "distinguished" faculty without offering salaries well above the academic scale, asking rhetorically: "Would you listen to a lecture on corporate finance or option pricing from someone earning less than a receptionist at an investment bank?" His viewpoint was that academic success ("as at Harvard and Stanford") can be attained "only through effective professional management of the institution"[23] Kay's successor, Anthony Hopwood, was able to claim that "It has now been accepted that the Said Business School should be in the intellectual and physical centre of the university."[24] When fifty years ago William Whyte looked to the future, he argued that inevitably and increasingly business school graduates would come to dominate the control of educational institutions, and so marginalise other subjects and other concerns. We believe that events at Oxford and elsewhere demonstrate that this has happened here. At the University of Luton, for example, the "repositioning strategy" to promote "popular and fashionable courses" in business and media has involved abandoning single-subject degrees in History, Modern Languages and Mathematics and the closure of the Humanities Faculty (which will be reconstituted, we are told, as a "creative industries department"). A third-year student of marketing supports such redefinition of what is meant by a university, saying "Luton should be known as a vocational university. On my course we don't write essays, we do business reports. All the teaching reflects what is happening in the real world."[25]

The redefining process has been intensified by recent changes in the climate of British universities, seen in government cutbacks in public funding, expansion in student numbers, an emphasis on "partnership", the ending of tenure for academics and the huge increase in limited-

23 John Kay, "Dream World" in *The Guardian*, 28 November 2000
24 Anthony Hopwood, "Modern Times", *The Guardian*, 5 December 2000
25 *The Guardian*, 19 May 2001

contract and part-time work. In the United States, the use of part-time faculty almost doubled between 1970 and 1993, according to the U.S. Department of Education, and now it has been calculated that almost half of the teaching positions in American higher education are part-time. In these circumstances, institutions have welcomed the approaches of banks, large companies and the Institute of Directors to endow chairs in management, marketing and business administration, to provide research funding and to initiate or subsidise "appropriate" research in these fields. The result has been both to increase the status and power of schools of management and to encourage their lecturers to give more time and attention to "consultancy" work as opposed to basic research and teaching.

The direct impact of "managerial" cultures on higher education institutions ("the McUniversities") is plain. We see it in the increased willingness of vice-chancellors to accept the role (or even the title in cases like Liverpool John Moores University) of chief executive, their readiness to appoint non-academics as senior managers, and their tendency to form small senior management teams, with delegated authority to take key decisions. We see it in the new emphasis on management skills and entrepreneurial ability in making appointments, and in the greater incentives for senior academics to be more "managerial". The higher that academics climb up the career ladder, the less time they give to students and teaching, the more to meetings and policy. When lecturers were asked recently whether bureaucracy had increased or decreased over the past three years, 95% said that it had increased. Our only surprise over this figure is to wonder where the other 5% were teaching. Asked about job satisfaction over the last two years, only 8% said that it had improved, as opposed to 54% who believed that it had deteriorated.[26]

26 *The Guardian*, 14 March 2000

As one illustration of this process we offer an advertisement for three new posts at the University of Lincolnshire & Humberside. Although we have little faith in ranking universities by league tables, it would be fair to say that this university rarely comes high, is sometimes alleged to have difficulties in recruiting students, and shares with other universities the general problems of maintaining academic standards. The University placed a lavishly illustrated half-page advertisement in the educational press, claiming "an international reputation as a dynamic and forward-looking, multi-site centre of learning", with this determinedly upbeat message:

INSPIRED BY THE CHALLENGE OF CHANGE
Faculty Manager (3 posts)

Your role will be to lead the delivery of an effective and efficient support service to a designated Faculty. You will actively contribute to the development, enhancement and implementation of administrative policies and practices, as well as provide management information which will support the strategic and business planning processes.

You will also be involved in the introduction of IT systems, financial management information and the production of publicity and publications, as well as performing a vital human resources management role.

With a degree or relevant postgraduate qualification, you will be able to demonstrate proven expertise in staff and change management with the ability to lead, motivate and achieve goals.

Your understanding of managerial processes will be matched by your energy, commitment and tenacity. You will also have highly developed planning, analytical and decision-making skills, together with the ambition to meet new challenges.[27]

It might reasonably be thought that a university anxious to better itself would first look to its teaching and research.

27 *The Guardian*, 12 October 1999

What would be the use of reaching strategic and business goals in a university if those goals were too broad, ill-defined and murky ever to attract and inspire good minds? What would be the purpose of applying an "efficient administrative support service" if the academic quality of all that it supports should be low? However, rather than seeking good teachers or researchers to cure their academic ills, the university advertises for three persons (at a combined cost of some £100,000 annually) with "proven expertise" in "change management" to "develop, enhance and implement" administrative policies and practices in the faculties to which they are, apparently at random, to be allotted.

Where does the drive come from? In the nineteen-eighties, there was a vogue in the United States for specialised books on university and college management (with titles like *Managing the Academic Enterprise, The Role of the Chief Academic Officer, Middle Management in Academe, The Market-Model University*). In the 'nineties, the word "management" became equally attractive for English publishers. One prestigious academic publisher offers guides for those working in Higher Education on "managing" almost everything: stress, strategy, human resources, quality, skills, equal opportunities, professional education and even management development itself. A new book from that press, *Making Managers in Universities and Colleges*, claiming to provide a "critically informed account of the repositioning of senior university and college academics as managers", was announced in these terms:

It [the book] is particularly concerned with the way "managing" involves the development of different ways of talking, acting and relating to people at work. Yet this is often difficult, and variably successful, as it confronts often strong professional and occupational work identities and cultures. The book provides a detailed look at the "manager" in contemporary further

and higher education in Britain as post-compulsory
education in Britain has been required to operate on a
more commercial basis, and universities and colleges
are increasingly regarded as small to medium sized
enterprises.[28]

The author could well claim that this is to describe the
situation as it is. However, the impersonalism of the
announcement is disturbing. Just who are the people who
regard universities as *enterprises* operating on a *commercial*
basis? Who *reposition* (or *make*) academics as managers (or
choose to reposition themselves in this way)? What will be
the personal costs of managing if it involves *relating* to
people and *acting* in new and different ways? If managerial
and professional attitudes *confront* each other, what will this
mean for the success of the institution?

The clash of values (a word notably absent from most
of these textbooks) is seen vividly in the way that *Total
Quality Management* (or its variant *Process Quality Management*)
has been implanted from business into the universities.
Pushed hard by governmental enthusiasm, it is perhaps the
most striking instance of management's penetration of
higher education. Just one of a number of recently fashionable industrial remedies, *TQM* is concerned with assuring
customers that the expected standards of a product will be
met consistently, using quality control and checks at appropriate stages in the production process. Surely nobody
doubts that universities should be concerned with the
quality of their work, but is the production-line *TQM*
model helpfully applicable? Who are the universities'
customers? What is their product? Who establishes standards, and how? What sort of consistency is possible and
desirable? Who should carry out quality control, and how?
To answer such questions in a *TQM* way means shifting the
emphasis away from those who teach towards those who

28 *New Books 2000* from the Open University Press, announcing Craig Pritchard,
Making Managers in Universities and Colleges, 2000

manage: establishing quality policies, producing "mission statements", proposing "benchmarks", agreeing standards for planning courses and assessing outcomes, setting up structures to monitor teaching and ensure compliance, or providing "appropriate" training. Those "managing" higher education simply *assumed* that *TQM* was appropriate, and in 1997 the *Quality Assurance Agency for Higher Education* was established. It proudly claims "to provide an integrated quality assurance service for higher education institutions throughout the UK", doing this "by visiting institutions to audit their overall academic management". Inevitably the *QAA* has a Mission Statement: "The Agency's mission is to promote public confidence that quality of provision and standards of awards in higher education are being safeguarded and enhanced." There is not much evidence to suggest that public confidence in the universities has been strengthened by the operations of the *QAA*. Indeed, all the management-inspired, government-promoted competitive "initiatives", known by acronyms like QAA, RAE (Research Assessment Exercise) and RTE (Research Transparency Exercise), imply that academics and universities cannot be trusted to govern themselves professionally. As one dissenting academic has argued, "The QAA's work is not about improving teaching: it is about controlling teachers."[29]

Departments are audited on their organisation, course documentation, policies and procedures. So—as happened in one of the universities in which the authors have worked—tutors are told that they must write "learning objectives" which avoid words like "know", "appreciate", or "understand", and substitute words like "label", "reproduce", "classify", "demonstrate" and "formulate"— the terminology of computers rather than of human beings. They are instructed: "Each learning objective

29 Bruce Charlton, "I Will Defy the Watchdog", *The Times*, 2 February 2000. Compare John Sutherland's attack on the damaging effects of the Research Assessment Exercise in *The Guardian*, 14 August 2000.

should be written as a separate statement which should be able to be evidenced at the end of the module", identifying "behaviour that has the potential to be observed". Just how does a student "evidence" for some impersonal observer that he or she has gained a subtler response to *King Lear*, a greater appreciation of a painting by Manet or a deeper understanding of Bach's *St Matthew Passion?* A genuine university education involves much more than "outcomes" that can be easily "evidenced" by compliant tutors, or short lists of separately stated "objectives" that can be ticked off and approved by state watchdogs. It is hard to avoid the conclusion that the overall influence of management schools upon our universities has been destructive, by dragging more solidly-based subjects to follow their own concentration on teaching only what is easily quantified, simply managed and readily "evidenced" and assessed.

Meanwhile the business schools themselves may be failing to harness the monster they have helped to loose upon the academic world. After attempts to revamp their syllabuses in the nineteen-nineties, they were again thrown into confusion by the collapse of the *dot.com* industries in the year 2000.

> In the last four years American business schools in particular have been hit by a technological whirlwind. The dot.com. boom and bust has been a catalyst for change . . . At UMBS, Dean Joseph B. White confirms that the new approach to teaching is just one impact of the new economy. "It has changed MBA programmes in multiple ways," he says. "It has had a huge career impact through changes in the curriculum. There is much more interest in entrepreneurial courses. In virtually all courses there is now a focus on the effects of new technology on the business . . . ."[30]

In Britain's universities the mood has been more sombre.

30 The MBA Supplement in *The Times*, 8 May 2001

There was a growing feeling that, having forced their colleagues to follow their music, the business schools had no clear understanding of the direction in which they should march. Their constantly shifting syllabuses were increasingly found irrelevant:

> ... most of it is little more than faddish quackery, remote from the question of how you eradicate foot and mouth, organise a rail system or keep your shops up to the mark. Management theory and the management consultants suffer from the same failings as the organisations they purport to advise.[31]

31 Will Hutton, "Thank Heavens for Sven", *The Observer*, 8 April 2001

5

eManaging the eArts

In a lecture at the newly-opened Royal Academy, the first President, Sir Joshua Reynolds, told his students: "If you have great talents, industry will improve them; if you have but moderate abilities, industry will supply their deficiency."[1] Reynolds was using the term "industry" in its original sense of "hard work" or "application". In the nineteenth century, during the process that became known as "the industrial revolution" the word acquired its later sense, that of "organised production". The factories of Britain, making tangible goods, were collectively titled "production industry". Then, in the middle of the twentieth century, the term "industry" once more began to shift its meaning, although the precise nature of the change was at first unclear. Raymond Williams noted:

The contrast between *industry* as factory production and other kinds of organised work was normal to mC20 and is still current. Yet since 1945, perhaps under American influence, *industry* has again been generalised, along the line from effort, to organised effort, to an institution. It is common now to hear of the *holiday industry*, the *leisure industry*, the *entertainment industry* and, in a reversal of what was once a distinction, the *agricultural industry*. This reflects the increasing capitalisation,

1 Sir Joshua Reynolds, *Discourses on Art*, Royal Academy, 1780 . One of the few books on this topic which can be recommended without qualification is Morris Eaves, *The Counter-Arts Conspiracy: Art and Industry in the Age of Blake*, Cornell University Press, 1992.

organisation and mechanisation of what were formerly thought of as *non-industrial* kinds of service and work.[2]

Yet there is plainly more to it than capitalistic organisation. The legitimate theatre for example was frequently capitalised, organised and mechanised in the same way as variety clubs or seaside halls, but in 1976 nobody had thought of including both within one "industry". Use of the word "industry", as in "film industry", still distinguished mass-market entertainment from the arts. Ten years previously a government White Paper, far from claiming that the arts were part of an industrial process or were useful lures for high-spending tourists, had been sternly dismissive of "those whose primary concern is with quantity and profitability".[3]

Although by the mid-seventies arts administrators had begun to realise that for politicians the single most important thing about the arts was their supposed economic value, most were still wary of leaving the real world of the arts for the more abstract realms of political economics. Typical was the guarded tone of the Arts Council of Great Britain's Annual Report 1973–4:

> There is of course a return from tourism. Travel advertisements in a number of countries say "Come to Britain for its arts and entertainment." . . . There is a return in the form of foreign currency, resulting from the visits of British companies and orchestras, singers and instrumentalists abroad.

Which is a long way from saying that the *prime reason* for supporting the arts is that they contribute to the national exchequer, and further still from saying that the arts constitute the whole or part of an "industry". Yet within a decade we were hearing that the arts were indeed part of a state-run "industry", and, like farming and the railways, in need of hard-nosed *modern management*. Those whose primary concern was "with quantity and profitability" were now

2 Raymond Williams, *Keywords*, Fontana Edn, 1976, p. 137
3 *Policy for the Arts: the First Steps*, HMSO, 1965

honoured rather than reviled, and, more significantly still, the state itself was becoming a cultural profiteer.

The big change came after 1979 in the first years of Mrs Thatcher's government. Now owners of stately homes, hoteliers, bus companies, tea shops, Chelsea pensioners, uniformed policemen, pillar boxes, morris dancers and Scotsmen wearing the kilt found themselves unexpectedly linked within the new state-created "tourist industry". Overlapping with it for a short time was a broadly-defined "leisure industry": music festivals, horse trials and golf clubs uneasily taking their places alongside the less rarefied pleasures of bingo, pop music and package holidays. Soon the "leisure industry" divided itself into its many parts—as the "hotel and catering industry", the "transport industry" and the "recreation industry". As the mysterious new "industries" multiplied in number, some businesses confusingly found themselves contributing to the output of several of them simultaneously. Pubs and restaurants for example, while naturally forming the backbone of the "hotel and catering industry", also played a significant part in the "tourist industry", the "hospitality industry" and the "holiday industry". Later, they also found time to make a valued contribution to the short-lived "arts industry" before finally coming to rest within Mr Smith's all-embracing "cultural" and "creative industries".

In its newest sense "industry" *seemed* just to mean "a political economy described and measured by bureaucrats". Certainly the new "industries" were unlike any previous industrial entity. They usually comprised a series of quite different enterprises, linked only in the minds of state planners, and not capitalised, organised or mechanised in any homogeneous way. Although they often belonged to the private sector, their economic "targets" were set by state officials, and regulated by state watchdogs. More confusingly still the boundaries of many of the new "industries" fluctuated by political whim, with the result that those working within them sometimes had to wait at the end of each year—as in the old Soviet Union—for the government statisticians to tell them whether they had done well or badly. Even then the published outcomes seemed to bear scant relationship to the world they knew. It was for example quite hard for those contemplating the decline of regional theatre, or the disappearance of instrumental music teaching from the state schools, nevertheless to be told that the government's "creative industries" were getting wealthier year on year and were in a constant state of well-funded expansion.

The public libraries offer a good example of the difficulty. As Britain entered—at least by its government's calculations—the third millennium, it seemed to be quite obvious that, whatever else was going along successfully, the national library service was in a bad way. Though one in three British adults still used public libraries, they were becoming harder to find, and when found harder still to find open. During the last decade of the twentieth century, nearly 150 of Britain's public libraries had closed. 80 % of the remainder had cut down their opening hours. At the same time the book purchasing power of all libraries had declined, in real terms, by some 12%. In February 2000 concerned writers lobbied parliament, urging members to take note of, and try to halt, the decline. One prolific author, Lady Antonia Fraser, was actually bold enough to suggest that if local authorities needed to make funding cuts, they should make them, not by cutting the library service, but by axing their own overpopulated bureaucracies.

The state managers had a ready answer. Like her fellow protesters, Lady Antonia was simply misinformed. In the same week that the protesting writers were pictured shuffling through the Westminster rain, a government conference was being held a couple of miles away which gave the official picture. This, in the opinion of *The Times*

(10.02.00), *proved* that the libraries were "Not a Cultural Backwater but a Creative Industry in full flow":

> A conference held this week at the British Library, entitled *Reading Tomorrow* and addressed by the Poet Laureate Andrew Motion and the Arts Minister Alan Howarth, proved that libraries are where it's at. Businesses—including Asda supermarkets and Ford Motor Company—have gone into imaginative partnerships with libraries and won over customers and enthused their staff.
>
> Government has recognised that libraries have power to change communities, that they are ideally placed to further its own declared goals of social cohesion, fostering the creative industries and providing access to education for all for life.

Exactly how this "creative industry in full flow" was going to achieve the government's own declared goals could not of course be spelled out in complete detail, but the conference was given some thrilling glimpses of the way things were going. "In Oldham," the *Times* report enthused, "the Dewey system was bypassed in favour of other methods of classification such as 'books about people more miserable than me'." Easy access to pulp fiction, *The Times* assured us, would "fuel the industry" (presumably by increasing the percentages of "library-users" amongst the semi-literate and literature-hating groups—a target which was also to be reached by using libraries as internet stations, tourist advice centres, coffee bars, souvenir shops and baby-changing facilities).

By the mid-'eighties the whole of the arts, at least in the eyes of government, was being transformed into an "industry". State subsidy was being given its new title of public *investment*. In 1988 the Policy Studies Institute, funded by the private Gulbenkian Foundation and a number of public bodies including the (then) Office of Arts and Libraries, the (then) Museums and Galleries Commission, the (then) Arts Council of Great Britain and the (then) Crafts Council, produced a 221-page report *The Economic Importance of the Arts in Britain.* This conveniently broadened the definition of the arts to include, for instance, all forms of music, and all kinds of published books and magazines. The report also included details of the supposed ancillary spending of arts-lovers, adding in what they spent in pubs and restaurants as being "arts-related" expenditure. At all events, by including previously-derided "profitable" activities within its remit, and counting in every possible element of travel and refreshment and other ancillary spending, the report was able to conclude that "the arts formed a significant economic sector in their own right", employing 496,000 people and with an annual turnover of £10 billion. Using similar accounting techniques the report concluded that "the arts are a major export earner for Britain, bringing in £4 billion a year."

The PSI report was followed shortly afterwards by a second, and even more bewildering document, which announced itself as a *National Arts and Media Strategy*, produced by the (then) Arts Council of Great Britain, the (then) British Film Institute and the (then) Crafts Council. The document was 60,000 words in length, of stupefying banality, revealing in every sentence the obvious unsuitability of its authors to pronounce upon the arts: "It is hard to discover an aesthetic language which carries the same weight as the 'hard facts' of attendance figures and invisible export earnings." (p. 5) On the contrary, it would be extremely hard to find a respectable aesthetic language which conveys so little of importance as does most political and economic jargon. In truth, these authors were incapable of *any* kind of aesthetic language. When they did want to seem to be saying something profound, they fell back on invented, quasi-political terms: "We believe that the development of cultural identity is a basic human need, alongside those for shelter, food and human relations."

(p. 10) Unfortunately the authors could not convey what they thought they meant by such phrases as "cultural identity", still less how government strategies could ensure that everybody developed one of them. For artists and arts administrators the "strategy's" chief value lay in its unwittingly artless exposition of the prevailing *zeitgeist*. It stood as a clear warning that state-created cultural "industries" are the inevitable harbingers of oppressive state management. As a contemporary commentator observed:

> The notion that the arts must now be regarded, solely and with no other purpose, as an *Industry*, is everywhere about us. Books, pictures, symphonies and plays are *products*; their readers, watchers and listeners merge into one hapless *consumer*, whose market habits are quantified by *arts marketers* so that they may be bribed into attending presentations which suit their *market needs*. Grants are no longer seen as a form of welfare, a disinterested concern for truth and beauty, but as *investments* which ultimately are *profitable* to the sponsors. No longer do critics search for the quality of the art, instead experts assess the *managerial efficiency* of any organisation which purports to control the distribution and sale of it. These experts now look to *minimise overheads*, carrying out *audits of current management practice* with *appraisal teams* and *monitoring committees* (all phrases, sadly enough, plucked from the current report of the British Arts Council) in which the concentration must, inevitably, be upon the bureaucratic, and never upon the pictures, plays and books. Artists are now judged by their *productive efficiency*, their *sales potential*, their *relevance to contemporary needs*. In other words, armament factories, sweetshops and arts centres are all to be judged by the same criteria; are the products competitively priced, and is there a lucrative market for them?
>
> This represents more than a mere change in terminology. People think as they say and write, and

behave as they think. The habitual use of the language of the bucket shop in the Arts Council's reports for example may have had some of its origins in a desire for self preservation ("talking to the government in the only language that it understands"), but it has now become ingrained in all that Arts Councils think, say and do.[4]

The techniques which were being employed were not evidence of fiendish conspiracies, which aimed to destroy the independent vigour of art and artists in Britain (though they often had that effect). Instead, governments claimed to be at the mercy of the "forces of change" unleashed by new information technology, and also claimed to be acting defensively against the all-encroaching battalions of the new global corporations. But whatever their motives, the bureaucratic steps in the creation of "industries" where none had existed before, soon became familiar. They are:

(a) Data is collected showing the economic size (and hence the political and "strategic" importance) of the target area.

(b) Areas for potential "development" (i.e. for change and control) are highlighted within it.

(c) The emerging "industry" is reorganised under new (state controlled) management, which takes over the central institutions in the field.

(d) The target area's aims, purposes and functions are redefined within the prevailing managerial language.

(e) The state assumes management of the target area by placing its own bureaucracy in control, setting its own "targets" and setting its own watchdog organisations to monitor its "development".

Sometimes these steps may be taken sequentially. At other times, as with the arts in Britain, they may occur more or

4 John Pick, "The Arts Industry" in *Journal of Arts Policy and Management*, City University, Vol. 3 No. 1, 1987

less simultaneously. For even as the PSI report was high-lighting key areas for "development" in the arts, the government was quietly moving against the existing arts institutions. Not one of the public institutions which had funded either the PSI report, or the writing of the "national strategy"—the Arts Council of Great Britain, the Regional Arts Boards, the Crafts Council, the Museums and Galleries Commission and the Office of Arts and Libraries—still survives intact. Some of those public institutions have simply disappeared. Others, like the Arts Council of Great Britain, have been broken up. Still others have had a change of name. But the remnants of nearly all of them disappeared during the early 'nineties into the same gaping bureaucratic maw—Britain's first-ever cultural ministry.

For decades the arts world had joined politicians in ridiculing the idea that Britain should ever create a government ministry for its culture. The monolithic brutality of Stalin's USSR, Mussolini's Italy and the Third Reich—all of which featured a Ministry of Culture—were, it was thought, too indelibly imprinted upon the British mind for this country ever to embark upon that course. We were too familiar with the crude methods these régimes employed:

> Italian Fascism commenced its cultural politics with a challenge to the structures of cultural display and distribution. The cultural bureaucracies and administrators of the Fascist dictatorship turned first to institutional reform, rather than promote or celebrate particular aesthetics or genres. The beginning years of Fascist cultural intervention, 1922–30, focused on government and party involvement in pre-existing institutions of high and mass culture, on the creation of new institutions where a lack was perceived, and on the professional organisation of cultural producers.[5]

Nevertheless, as soon as pre-existing cultural institutions

5 Maria Susan Stone, *The Patron State: Culture and Politics in Fascist Italy*, Princeton, 1998, p. 23

had been broken up, or had their effectiveness blunted by forcing them to converse in the deadening language of modern management, the new British Ministry began its reign. The Department of National Heritage, as it was called in its early days, opened in 1992. There was no pretence that it had been called into being for any pressing historical, cultural or academic reason. It existed in the form that it did wholly for bureaucratic convenience, so that there could be effective state management of the eclectic list of activities that were now deemed to be the "national heritage", but also because the government wished to standardise and "develop" this new parcel of "industries". The newly-titled Minister for National Heritage, Peter Brooke, broke the news of the government's real intentions in his Foreword to the Ministry's first annual report:

It is a pleasure to introduce the first departmental report of the Department of National Heritage. It provides a detailed account of the achievements of 1992, the first year of the Department's existence; and it looks ahead over the next three years to 1995–6.

The Department of National Heritage[6] was formed in April 1992 and has responsibility for the arts, museums and galleries, libraries, the heritage, film, sport, tourism, broadcasting, the Press and the National Lottery. They were formerly the responsibility of six other Departments.

The work involved in bringing these functions together in a single Department at the same time as tackling major new policy developments has meant that this has been an extremely busy year. But I am confident that the Department is now well-established and able to face the challenges in the years to come. The formation of the new Department represents a unique

6 Calling it the *National* Heritage was stretching it a bit. It didn't, for example, include gardening, still the nation's most popular leisure activity, presumably because in peacetime the activity offers little scope for government intervention.

opportunity to build successfully upon many great achievements in the areas that it covers.

Well might artists have quailed at this! The old Office of Arts and Libraries through which the defunct Arts Council of Great Britain had received its annual subvention had always been careful to say that *responsibility* for the arts did not rest with them, but with artists and the Arts Council. The new Ministry not only *covered* the arts (and broadcasting, sport and the heritage) but assumed *responsibility* for them. This did not mean that it intended, as in totalitarian states, to assume full financial responsibility for their operation. What it did mean however was that the new body was going to use the same control techniques as had the ministries of the totalitarian régimes. Though largely composed of elements of the private sector, the arts were henceforward going to be treated as a state-run *industry*, whose major purposes were to promote a forward-looking image of New Britain and to make a sound contribution to the national economy.[7] The new Ministry would standardise reporting of "the arts industry", and would evaluate and control it by means of its quantifying managerial jargon. There was a fairly clear hint that this process was beginning in that same report:

> One distinctive characteristic of the Department of National Heritage is that it operates very largely through a network of public bodies and agencies which receive much of their support through public funds but which are managed and operate at arm's length from government. These bodies, which are widely different in size and function, were formerly the responsibility of other Government Departments which had adopted various styles of annual reporting. In this report, *we have begun the task of reporting the activities of these bodies on a consistent basis*, while reflecting something of their

7 In a "key policy statement" in 1998 Mr Smith said that the arts must deliver results "in line with the government's wider objectives".

heterogeneity, and shall make further progress on this for the 1994 report. [our italics]

The arts world can have had little inkling of how rapid that bureaucratic progress was going to be. Nor can they have realised how powerfully its growth would be fuelled by the advent of a new and malign power, which had for nearly two centuries been unthinkable as an ally of the British government. The new National Lottery was in its final stages of planning when the Ministry was created and, in spite of the fact that it was plainly destructive of much of the British cultural heritage, the DNH proudly adopted it.

A further defining moment in the industrialisation of British culture came a year and more before the 1997 election, when the then opposition leader, Tony Blair, made an extended visit to Australia to barter with Rupert Murdoch over the way New Labour would be presented in the Murdoch media. During his visit Mr Blair became enamoured of a cultural policy which had recently been put into practice by Keating's Labour government, called *Creative Nation*. The essence of this was to redefine the arts as just one species of "creative commodity" (along with such profitable activities as blockbuster films, the fashion industry and computer games), then to map the trade this new sector generated, and finally to make government subventions at those points at which the newly-designated "creative industries" were deemed likely to yield most profit to the nation. In economic terms the policy was merely specious, but in artistic and critical terms, it was disastrous. It took no account of the realms in which the arts actually existed, merely noticing their supposed economic "outcomes". It stretched the meanings of terms like "creativity" and "cultural development" well beyond legitimate bounds, and after a period of three or four years, as the policy began to implode, it was found to have harmed both the arts and the critical understanding of art. It did not survive the Keating government.

But it had greatly impressed Mr Blair. When he flew home from Australia he ordered his then shadow Minister for National Heritage, Jack Cunningham, to drop the plans Labour had painstakingly drawn up in opposition, and instead to copy Australia's "big idea". On taking office after the election, Blair appointed the shadow Health Minister Chris Smith to National Heritage, and asked for implementation of a large "Creative Nation" policy on the admired Keating model. Smith duly thought big. He immediately increased the size of his Ministry, increased its Ministerial representation in the Commons, and, shortly afterwards, went the whole hog and announced that the government agency he had inherited would henceforward be known by the title Hitler and Stalin had both favoured—the Ministry of Culture.[8]

The British Ministry of Culture intended, it would seem, to be no less prescriptive than its totalitarian forebears, and the arts now found themselves in strange company. As Mr Smith explained in *The Times* (04.10.97), the national culture now included everything from the Royal National Theatre to the national lottery:

> The Department's interests cover the spectrum of life in Britain, from the popular culture of music, television *and the drama of the lottery draw* to those areas of the arts which, in Matthew Arnold's classic definition of culture are "a pursuit of total perfection by means of getting to know. . . 'the best which has been thought and said in the world'."[our italics]

As a direct consequence of this, those artists, teachers and critics who had been genuinely concerned with pursuing excellence, the "best which has been thought and said", now found that they were mentioned less and less in

---

8 The full title of the new body was "The Department of Culture, Media and Sport". As "Culture" was now a political term, and as its "targets" seemed always to involve economic growth and employment, it seemed inevitable that the Ministry must one day be subsumed within the Department of Trade and Industry.

national debates, and that the arts had been all but dissolved within the murky soup of the "creative industries". Within these new state industries consideration of artistic excellence had only a marginal place. Excellence now involved modern management, slick marketing, high sales figures and playing one's part in promoting the approved "national identity". As one of the successes of the new "creative industries", Tracey Emin, commented with characteristic grace: "One thing is for sure, you're not going to make it as an artist if you don't understand commerce and you're working in an attic for 20 years, slagging off people like me and complaining about never being discovered."[9]

The opportunities for "making it as an artist" were however greater than ever, for you could now make it in any one of a satisfying number of commercial fields. According to Mr Smith the "creative industries" by 1998 contained almost every legal activity which involved large sums of money, including Advertising, Architecture, Art and Antiques, Computer Games ("The UK computer-games industry is ranked among the very best in the world, and the global market is growing rapidly . . ."), Crafts, Design, Designer Fashion ("The UK fashion industry has an importance and prominence out of proportion to its size . . . ."), Film, Music, Performing Arts, Publishing, Software, and Television and Radio ("Despite the fact that exports have doubled in the last ten years, there is a growing trade deficit as more and more imports are drawn in by the multi-channel packages").

Mr Smith's 1998 book *Creative Britain*, which for the most part comprised the text of lectures he had given in the gilded *salons* of the capital, said all the expected things about the importance of culture, of creative activity and the need for the best things to be generally accessible. The tone is sometimes maudlin. "No-one," he said to his

9 *The Observer*, 30 January 2000

audience at the London Playhouse on 19 September 1997, "who has lived through the last three tragic weeks here in Britain [following the death of Diana, Princess of Wales] can doubt . . . that there is such a thing as a national cultural sense. . . . What we have witnessed, I believe, is a real feeling that we are coming together as a nation, in shared grief but in shared purpose too." Sometimes the tone is preachy. "The arts are not optional extras for government," he informed fellow-diners at the Royal Academy on 22 May 1997, "they are at the very centre of our mission." "Anyone looking into a society from the outside," he averred on 1 December 1997 in the Connaught Rooms, London, "whether geographically or with the benefit of historical hindsight—will regard the artistic and cultural life of that society as a barometer of its health. It is one of the main factors by which we assess a civilisation." He went earnestly on,

> And it is a tenet that does not just recognise the importance of culture of itself. It also recognises the importance of ensuring that the widest possible number of people can have access to that cultural excellence. If I had to encapsulate the central theme of our new Government's approach to the arts, it would be this, our aim is to make things of quality available to the many, not just the few.

"Let us," he exhorted an audience of Royal Academicians, "make such exclusivity a thing of the past."

Unfortunately almost everything else that Mr Smith said and did militated against those high-sounding sentiments. And elsewhere in that same book he so determinedly mixed real artists with the second-rate, so harped upon their market successes and made it so clear that every element of British cultural life had a primary duty to promote the positive rebranding of Britain, that one was bound to question his oft-repeated commitment to quality, and *artistic* excellence:

Although the UK represents only about 7% of the total world market for sound recordings, around 25% of all records sold worldwide have a British element—be it artist, songwriter or record company. UK artists currently enjoying significant success in the US include not only the ubiquitous Spice Girls, but Seal, Enya (Irish, but signed to a UK company), Oasis, the Prodigy, Jamiroquai and UB40, all of whom have joined consistently popular artists such as Phil Collins and Elton John in selling many millions of records in the United States. (22 October 1997)

And he repeatedly slipped from talking about "the freedom" of artists and local communities to make their own choices, to an insistence that all free Britons must henceforward operate *within* a state-determined "strategy"— one which, according to Mr Smith, involved embracing information technology, and getting rid of old-fashioned books, so that we could better live in an "information society":

> I am . . . conscious of the potential for conflict between the Government's desire to develop the library service as a platform for delivering wider policy objectives, and the vital principle of local determination that underlies public-library provision. . . . The way of squaring this particular circle is to develop an overall national strategy within which local library authorities can operate. . . . It must develop the links that exist between libraries and other sectors. And it must allow libraries to grasp the nettle in harnessing information technology. In short, it must ensure that libraries form part of the bedrock of the developing information society. (23 September 1997)

Mr Smith meanwhile continued to enlarge his cultural bureaucracy. A new Film and Media Board soon took its place alongside the restructured Arts Council of England, and was in turn joined by the National Endowment for

Science, Technology and the Arts, one of whose major purposes was bluntly admitted to involve turning "creativity into products and services which we can exploit in the global market".

Yet another bureaucracy, this time bearing the uneasy title of the Creative Industries Taskforce, which brought together leaders of the "creative industries" with representatives from the Treasury, the Department of Trade and Industry, the Foreign Office and the Department of Education and Employment, was set up by the new government. It was given the task of "mapping" (i.e. deciding the content, and aggrandising the economic significance of) the newly-widened "creative industries". Its first estimates put the size of these new industries at over £50 billion, but this figure, bloated as it seemed, was only a sighting shot. In 1998 the Department put out a 112-page "Mapping Document" which had already raised the figure to "nearly £60 billion"—which seemed to be an open invitation for everyone who was not already employed as a consultant in the creative industries to become a compiler of further "creative industries" data, and to shovel more artgeld into the ministerial bucket.

It was one of modern management's finest hours. New bureaucracies sprang up everywhere, concerned not just with the cultural and creative "industries", but with every kind of notional "economic regeneration". In their own terms the new managers were busy and purposeful, but when any of their managerial documents fell into the hands of sceptical observers, it seemed that they inhabited a world of uneasy self-delusion. Reactions of a disinterested observer to any such "mission statement" were likely to include bewilderment at its general vacuity, mild irritation over its quasi-military acronyms, and considerable unease at the apparently limitless political ambition such documents always seemed to express. For it seemed that the desire to assemble information about the national culture invariably led to a desire to assess and evaluate it, which in turn gave way to a consuming desire to *control* it. Some hint of all this may be gleaned from the literature which one such state-funded body, the *Cultural Business Support for South Yorkshire Unit*, put out in 1999:

> Previously known as the Cultural Industries Development Unit, the organisation has run bespoke business support and training for the creative sector during the Pilot programme from July 1996 to November 1997. This was managed and funded by a steering group: Sheffield TEC, Sheffield City Council, Business Link Sheffield and the Cultural Business Network. During the Pilot Phase the organisation successfully delivered to over 300 individuals and SMEs. There followed a period of project appraisal and development planning, funded by SRB, ERDF and the Local Authority in 1998. Since the formation of a constituted non-profit company in June 1998, ACT has negotiated for resources and commissioned project management to set up a staffed unit, with in-kind time given by the board and advisers, and a dedicated project champion working part-time and funded by the Local Authority.

The aim of this tiny bureaucracy may not be immediately apparent to the uninitiated reader. But it seems that it was nothing less than to "create a world class centre of excellence in the creative industries" in South Yorkshire.

The first step towards this goal was running a programme of modern management training for the locals, including "Entrepreneurship", "Management", "Finance" and "Presentation and Negotiation Skills". Nowhere in the Unit's gritty documentation were the arts, or even creativity, considered in any kind of detail—the assumption seemed to be that kind of thing, unlike *strategising* and *modern management techniques*, could take care of itself. The one segment of the Unit's training programme which might be suspected of being concerned with what artists did—grandly termed *Cultural Experience*—turned out to be concerned above all with ensuring that all local activity was fully enmeshed within the state bureaucracy. In all there were four activities which were to lead the organisation towards global domination:

• Develop bespoke training programmes for the subsidised arts sector in association with Yorkshire Arts Board
• Assist non-profit and voluntary sector arts organisations with funding sources and bids.
• Deliver Board Development programmes and links between business and the funded Arts sector in association with ABSA North and Business in the Arts.
• Establish links with Lottery programmes, NESTA, New Opportunities Fund, Awards for All and European programmes to ensure maximum impact on local artistic and creative sector.

This unit is of course no worse than dozens of others, and (for one cannot know what criteria are now used to determine "world-class centres of excellence" in the "creative industries") one day it may achieve its chosen managerial objectives. We merely observe that this ambitious little bureaucracy, proselytising for the new Ministry's top-down support systems, preaching the virtues of modern management, yet operates within shouting distance of one of the most public failures of the whole "creative industries" frenzy. Sheffield's National Centre for Popular Music had impeccable credentials—heavily funded by the state lottery, its management and marketing put in place by some of the best-paid consultants in the industry—but it has not been, to put it politely, an outstanding success.[10]

It would of course be unfair even to mention this, still

---

10 The £15 million centre opened in March 1999. Its consultants, Coopers and Lybrand, had conducted research which showed that the actual attendance would be

less to draw from it any conclusions, were it not generally the case that Britain's new cultural managers constantly tell us that everything is in fact going *extremely* well. Let us briefly glance by way of illustration at one of the most visible of the state-managed cultural institutions, the Royal Opera House. Its renovation has been the largest of the lottery-funded projects, with a capital grant of more than £60 million. Its reopening in late 1999, in greatly enlarged premises, was under a new American executive director. This event followed upon a year's closure (during which, uniquely, the company had retained its full Arts Council grant-in-aid for giving performances). The Minister had taken a close personal interest both in the restructuring of the management and in the House's new philosophy. It was to open on time, within budget, and henceforth to be known as the "People's Opera House". The one managerial target that was clearly met was that the rebuilt opera house did open on time—though with a platform performance of opera highlights and an understandably cautious performance by the dance company (much of the back-stage equipment was not ready for operation). But it was already £7 million over budget. Worse was to follow, as the technical difficulties meant that in the first month no fewer than twelve performances were cancelled. And there was no sign that it had been transformed into a "People's Opera House". Indeed the reopening night was one of the most starry events that fashionable London had seen for some time, black-tie save for the Minister, who reputedly salved his political conscience by wearing a dark red bow. The management then received a barrage of complaints from those who had paid heavily for seats from which there was a poor view, followed by another wave of

around 400,000 a year, with a "worst case" scenario of 300,000. In the event, up to the end of 1999, it had slightly fewer than 100,000 visitors. By that time it had already run up debts of over £1 million, and 20 out of its 50 staff had lost their jobs. Later, it closed. It was not South Yorkshire's only failure. The "Earth Centre" at Doncaster attracted fewer than half of its forecast number of visitors in its first year of operation.

complaints from those who wished to wander through its state-financed foyers, but frequently found them closed off for "corporate events".

None of which would have been out of the way— newly-built theatres and opera houses notoriously have technical problems, after all—were it not for the manic desire of the cultural spin-doctors to pretend that all was well. "Let's dream again," said Michael Kaiser, the executive director, in a *Times* interview at the end of that first disastrous month, "We're about art, so let's dream about art. It's very uplifting to be in that mode."[11] In the course of the ensuing conversation the interviewer observed that while in that etherial mode Mr Kaiser talked neither with artists nor people—but to himself:

> We're treated as a government agency, so people expect a service from us, but at the same time we have to go out and raise private money. Is it a balancing act? Sure. Do we let donors pick our art in return for support? No, we don't. Have there been mistakes? I guess. Are we constantly readjusting? Of course.

For Mr Kaiser's language is particularly well suited to modern management. Mistakes are discussed in the abstract, something there may have "been". The remedial forces are, however, personalised. It is they—the managers—who are seeing this through on your behalf. But it is an inappropriate language for the arts. While it would be reasonable for the management of British Telecom to say that they are "constantly readjusting", the same phrase in the mouth of an opera house director savours too much of manipulation, implying that the major concern is for effective packaging and slick marketing rather than for artistry.

For, in spite of all that modern politicians may do and say, the arts are *not* an industry. As one commentator recently observed:

11 *The Times*, 30 January 2000

Economic and artistic success do not necessarily coincide. The business-strategies of arts-producing organisations tend to be distinct from those of commercial producers, "emergent" rather than "deliberate". Sales can increase and prices can rise not because of huge marketing efforts but simply because of an artist's growing reputation. The imposing quantitative statistics for "growth" in the arts studiously ignore questions of quality. The many surveys of people attending theatres or concerts say nothing at all about the merits of what is being seen or heard, or the nature of the response made by individuals to their experience.[12]

In the final count, the most comprehensive map of the "creative industries" will not tell us where we may find "creativity" occurring, for in the context of government pronouncements it is, like "modern management", merely a bureaucratic construct. Nor will the most intensive "mapping" help us to rediscover art, or criticism. What we can say is that in a healthy culture, in which the arts were established by common judgement rather than by state directive, neither the "creative industries" nor the "cultural industries" could possibly exist.

---

12 Robert Protherough, "Is Culture an Industry?", *The Kenyon Review*, Vol. XXI, 1999, Nos 3/4

6

Managing the Schools

Before 1970 books on school management hardly existed; nowadays the library shelves are heavy with them. Educational management may only have "become a discrete discipline during the last twenty-five years or so,"[1] but in that time it has swiftly shifted from the periphery to the centre. In 1987 the first issue of *Management in Education* appeared, bearing the imprint of the British Educational Management and Administration Society. Courses on management for teachers have been given increasing governmental priority (trebling in funding between the late 'eighties and the early 'nineties) and inevitably are now perceived by schools themselves as their dominant need. The almost automatic assumption seems to be that if schools are weak, or in current jargon "failing", then this must be the result of poor management. Education texts of the nineteen-nineties show in their chapter and section headings that "the importance of whole school management" is an article of faith that apparently no longer needs justification. One well-regarded volume assumes that its teacher-readers will be looking for "reasons for seeking promotion [*sic*] to a management post", and offers tips on "how to pursue a career in management". It considers "the urgent need for middle management training", "the problems caused by managers' lack of training", the key "management skills" and "management styles". But

1 Patrick Whitaker, *Managing Schools*, Oxford, 1998, p. xii

particularly interesting is the implicit ideology, suggesting that management is largely to do with shifting reluctant teachers in the direction *you*, the manager, wish them to go. So sections deal with "motivating older, more experienced or disaffected colleagues" and "reducing resistance to change". The conclusion begins with the words: "The need for training and yet more training for middle managers is my major conclusion." It is no great surprise that the author describes himself as a freelance management consultant in education and industry.[2]

When we were directly involved in the work of secondary schools in the 'fifties and early 'sixties we accepted unquestioningly that they were essentially self-contained bodies run by teams of teachers. A head—also a practising teacher—might be supported by a deputy, who would be teaching virtually a full timetable. The rest of the staff were full-time teachers, who also ran out-of-school activities at lunchtimes and in the afternoons, who arranged visits and accompanied school teams to matches on Saturdays. Administration—staff-meetings, reports, parents' evenings—was fitted in wherever room could be found for it. We do not look back on this period through a golden haze of nostalgia. Then, as now, there were excellent schools, poor schools, and everything in between. But, as a matter of fact, that world is gone; schools and the roles that teachers play in them have changed radically in thirty years or so. One reason that industrial-style management theory invaded the schools so swiftly was simply because school management had not previously been seen as a separate or significant concern; good teachers were already good managers.

According to the spate of guides and handbooks, what are the areas in which "effective" (a favourite word) or "quality" school management operates today? As one volume asks: "What do education managers need to be

2 Quotations from Jack Dunham, *Developing Effective School Management*, 1995

good at?"[3] The answers advanced there seem to be that they are the management of learning and the curriculum, assessment, financial resources, legislative requirements, staff relationships (including appointments and promotion), teacher appraisal, professional development, the handling of stress, students' entitlement, promotion of the school's image and identity, and so on. Nobody is likely to dissent from this. However, all these topics were equally the concern of those heads and teachers working in the schools of the 'fifties and 'sixties that we have briefly described. Teachers then handled them in different ways and with different degrees of success as part of their normal, accepted professional work. Nobody at that stage suggested that these functions should be siphoned off and put in the hands of a special, select group. Now the redefining of the roles of heads and senior staff is perceived by teachers as driving a wedge between "managerial" staff and "teaching" staff. Managerialism in the hands of a few undermines the professionalism of the many.

> For heads and teachers their respective roles in meeting National Curriculum requirements are transformed from being those of professionals, more bound by their common professional membership, than divided by their rank, to those of manager and managed.[4]

At the national level, the Secretary of State for Education has now become a super-manager, with virtually unlimited power to form policy and to compel its implementation. In place of the voluntary and elected bodies of the past we have hand-picked groups to ensure compliance. Money that could be spent on the education service is increasingly deployed to push forward ministerial whim.

3 Lesley Kydd, Megan Crawford and Colin Riches, (eds), *Professional Development for Educational Management*, Open University Press, Milton Keynes, 1997, p. 87

4 R. Ferguson, "Managerialism in Education" in L Clarke *et al.*, *Managing Social Policy*, 1994. See the chapter by Lucy Bailey on how teachers talk about their work and the one on "Restructuring the Governance of Schools: the impact of managerialism on schools in Scotland and England" in Margaret A. Arnott and Charles D. Raab (eds), *The Governance of Schooling*, 2000.

Government bodies with frequently changing acronyms are set up to dictate curriculum and assessment. An enormous testing mechanism is established to ensure that schools teach to this imposed curriculum. Thousands of inspectors are expensively recruited to assess the effectiveness of schools and teachers. Other bodies (with yet more inspectors) are established to oversee the education of teachers in training. When the blame (for poor management, of course) is directed at Local Education Authorities, then yet more consultants have to be hired at great cost to sort them out and—as in Leeds—schools can find themselves "outsourced" to a "joint venture company". For over quarter of a century schools have been bombarded with government "initiatives", at times more than twenty of them in a year, that they are expected to support. The assumption of both Conservative and Labour governments has been that they know best, and that their changes (often called "reforms") automatically equal improvement. The 1998 Green Paper was typically called *Meeting the Challenge of Change* and when a new Secretary of State was appointed after the 2001 election her first message was all about the need for managing still more change. Her talk of "new agenda" and "transformation" indicated just another stage in the cumulative process that has resulted in teaching being more oppressively "managed" from above than at almost any time in the past.

How have these changes come about? The first major managerial restructuring came almost unnoticed with the wholesale swing to comprehensive education. The most common pattern for reorganisation was for two or three existing schools to be amalgamated, either on a new site or on the enlarged "home" of one of them. These new schools faced the problem of what has been called the "second marriage syndrome" (where the happy couple find themselves with two refrigerators, two washing machines, two cookers and so on). What was to happen when two or three people from different schools had all been called Head of English or Head of Mathematics? Their salaries were secure; their status had to be maintained. The almost universal answer was to create new roles and new structures. Those who did not gain the "academic" appointments were made Heads of House or Heads of Year, with Deputies to support them. And fearing that these "pastoral" roles might lack academic prestige, those who were appointed were given reduced teaching timetables and managerial responsibilities over groups of staff and students. The school then had to operate with a double structure and twin lines of command. Most teachers suddenly found themselves responsible both to a subject head of department and to a pastoral head of house or year.

Those who taught in schools throughout this time have remarked to us on the way in which paperwork and committee meetings multiplied—not always for any clear purpose—as the pastoral sector swiftly became the administrative arm of "senior management" —a term that then began to be fashionable. Once these posts had been created there was no way in which such a promising channel for promotion could be abolished. Subject teachers had to work harder and harder to support the growing number of those whose chief interests lay outside the classroom. With all these senior staff, it soon seemed necessary for a head to be supported by three deputies, and sometimes also by bursars, office managers and counsellors. New hierarchies were established, and the days in which successful classroom teachers might become heads without taking on some intervening "managerial" role vanished. Heads themselves frequently became too busy to teach and spent increasing amounts of time outside their schools. Their deputies retired to offices to control their designated "areas": curriculum, timetable, staff development, student affairs, or even "public relations". Once it was said that you could recognise teachers by their sports jackets with leather patches on the elbows; now members of the "senior management team" started to separate themselves by their dark suits and silk ties, going off to comfortable hotels at the week-end for "bonding sessions".

The other significant adoption of managerial theory and practice, which came from above and from a different political direction, can only be understood by placing it briefly in context. Nearly a century ago, the Board of Education published two major reports[5] that established a long tradition for defining and managing educational policy. The first of these disclaimed any intention "to frame a syllabus of instruction or to prescribe in detail the methods by which teachers should proceed", suggesting that to do so would be both useless and harmful. Schools and teachers differed so materially that "no external authority can or ought to offer detailed guidance. General principles must be translated into practice by the teacher." The following year, the second report stressed the dangers of expecting teachers to "follow a syllabus which they have not worked out for themselves" particularly if they are "not at liberty to teach this syllabus in their own way". In such a situation, the teacher "surrenders the role of an educator and becomes a 'crammer'." A tacit convention was thus established that there would be no central prescription of curriculum or methodology. Teachers were to decide for themselves how to implement agreed general principles. For many years education ministers of different parties acted in such an "arms-length" way upon professional advice, essentially rubber-stamping the administrative proposals put forward by the Ministry or Department and by the Inspectorate. From today's standpoint, it seems almost incredible that heads and teachers were allowed to get on with their work autonomously with so little outside interference.

5 *The Teaching of English in Secondary Schools*, HMSO, 1910; *Report of the Consultative Committee on Examinations in Secondary Schools*, HMSO, 1911 (The Dyke Acland Report)

Changes came swiftly and became increasingly political. At first the arguments were largely about structure. There were vigorous debates about the relative merits of comprehensive and selective systems, about the advantages of unified rather than separate examinations, and about the appropriate school leaving age. Then public and political attention shifted towards the curriculum—what should be taught and how—which had previously been seen as a wholly professional matter. At the end of the sixties, the frankly polemical *Black Papers* (edited by Cox and Dyson), criticising academic standards and teaching methods in comprehensive schools, helped to stimulate debate but also created an almost hysterical suspicion of schools and teachers that was rapidly pushed forward by the popular press. The climate was ripe for more direct political intervention. This is generally seen as dating from the speech of James Callaghan at Ruskin College, Oxford, in October 1976, initiating the so-called *Great Debate* over education policy, directly linking the activities of schools to the country's economic performance and the needs of society. The assumption that education was somehow failing in these respects and a growing suspicion of teachers' professionalism were seen as justifying management from the top. Within a decade fifteen major documents had issued from the Department or from the Inspectorate detailing (often conflicting) views of how schools should be organised and the curriculum reshaped.

In the 1980s Sir Keith Joseph started to use the formal powers that had been left in abeyance by his predecessors in order to curtail discussions with professional groups and to formulate policy from the top through legislation. Instead of referring to the *administration* of schools the government chose to speak of their *management*. This symbolic shift marked a determination to move away from professional self-regulation to externally imposed criteria and the play of "market forces" (which Sir Keith used to justify a dubious distinction between "useful" and other subjects). Between 1978 and 1996, the proportion of the UK's educational budget being spent centrally more than doubled. New competence-based qualifications (significantly implemented through the Department of Employment rather than of Education) laid great emphasis on rigid models of industrial management. Teachers began to be defined as "operatives" rather than as professionals. Sir Keith's 1983 White Paper on *Teaching Quality*[6] was pervasively vague about what that quality was thought to be or how it was manifested, but it was very precise about the managerial and legislative changes that Sir Keith believed (without citing any evidence) would bring about improvement. The hard-nosed utilitarianism of the language was full of references to "cash plans", "supply and demand", "shrinkage", and the need to "moderate growth" (and, indeed, public spending on education fell by 10% in real terms in the next seven years). The White Paper's models were those of industrial management. It was for the government to decide which courses should be "allowed to continue"; teachers would be assessed according to certain centrally laid-down criteria for "appraisal of competence", and "employers" would be responsible for cutting back their "labour force" by employing "management tools . . . such as compulsory redundancy", "planned redeployment" and "short term contracts".

Later that year (in the *Curriculum Matters* series) Sir Keith emphasised his determination to control what teachers taught in schools as an imposed "guaranteed" curriculum. These measures radically changed the nature of teaching in ways that have continued and developed to the present day. The only surprise, in view of what was to happen three years later, is that in 1985 any ideas of a national curriculum seemed to be firmly rejected. In the last gasp of

6 Advisory Committee on the Supply and Education of Teachers, *Teaching Quality*, HMSO, 1983

the traditional policy, teachers were assured that "curriculum development is a professional activity", and that "it would not be right" for the Secretary of State to introduce legislation imposing national syllabuses.[7]

This decision was promptly revoked by Kenneth Baker, Sir Keith's successor, who used the powers of his office to make "agreed national objectives" mandatory, claiming that the curriculum was "too important to be left to teachers". His 1988 Education Act was a deliberate attempt to reshape the accepted form of educational control in Britain. Baker saw the existing structure of checks and balances as ambiguous and an obstacle to having his own way, so he set about dismantling it. His Act gave him more than 400 new powers. As well as making parliament the arbiter of what should be taught, the government encouraged schools (and eventually colleges and polytechnics) to opt out of local authority control through the Local Management of Schools (Devolved School Management in Scotland). The policy of what became known (inaccurately) as "parental choice" weakened the role of local authorities over admissions to schools (and the Inner London Education Authority was abruptly abolished). In a 1999 interview with Nick Davies, Lord Baker looked back with pleasure on the success of his strategy, admitting that all the measures had "a political edge, though no one admitted it".

> He knows a lot of people tried to say he was just settling political scores, that his real agenda was to punish the teacher unions and to kill off the local education authorities; that secretly the big master plan was to wipe out comprehensive schools by stealth. And now he's laughing because the funny thing is—they were right! "I took away all negotiating rights from the union. It was quite brutal." He chuckles as he recalls how by statute he removed their right to negotiate . . .

7 DES, *Better Schools*, HMSO, 1985, par. 85

And the LEAs generally—"I put them on the course to slowly wither on the vine." He makes no apology for this. "I have no regrets.". . . But did he realise that the introduction of "parental choice" would polarise the system and effectively kill off the comprehensives? "Oh, yes. That was deliberate".[8]

Baker's attack on the comprehensives, by combining parental "choice" with his new funding formula dependent on recruitment, polarised the difference between schools which gathered the brightest children and the most funds (effectively like grammar schools) and the contemporary equivalent of secondary modern schools, in poor areas, with disadvantaged children struggling on a reduced budget. In keeping with the market ideology of the government, this was presented as devolving power from the "producers" (teachers and teacher unions in particular, local authorities, advisers and what were called disparagingly "educationists") towards the "customers" (assumed without debate to be the parents of schoolchildren). Despite the free market rhetoric, however, these customers were given no say about management of the National Curriculum, which was firmly centralised in the hands of the Secretary of State. Indeed, perhaps the strangest aspect of the speedy introduction of the National Curriculum was the lack of any significant rationale for the form it took or any way of monitoring its effectiveness. The choice of "core", "foundation" and "other" subjects in that curriculum, the divisions between them and the possible places left for citizenship, sex education, politics, and the arts were highly debatable and largely arbitrary (it was said that Kenneth Baker jotted down the subjects for his curriculum on the back of an envelope). In fact, the structure hardly differed at all from that of the 1904 Secondary Regulations.

The imposing style of its launching led some teachers to expect an authoritative and almost permanent statement

8 *The Guardian*, 16 September 1999

of principles and practice that all teachers could follow. What happened demonstrated how misguided they were. It swiftly became impossible to talk of *the* National Curriculum as something definitive. Within five years, three irreconcilable versions of *a* National Curriculum for English had been promulgated (together with an additional variant for Wales) and four committees or working parties had been charged with drafting or revising these documents without ever reaching consensus. Consequently, at regular intervals teachers were expected to change their practice not on the basis of their professional understanding but because the views of management kept shifting. The long tradition of "guidance" (however heavy-handed) had given way to straightforward prescription. Power was placed in the hands of "advisory" committees, hand-picked by the Secretary of State to ensure that only one viewpoint was ultimately heard. The independent inspectorate (HMI) was abolished and replaced by the Office of Standards in Education, firmly within the hands of politicians.[9]

Teachers have seen a significant shift in balance away from the classroom, not only in such direct governmental intervention but also in the indirect pressures on school cultures: the greater power given to school management, the control of budgets and of in-service provision, the perceived need for schools to "compete", the emphasis on "market values" (with sponsored teaching materials carrying advertisements)—all tending to remove objectives, policy, resourcing from the hands of classroom teachers. Their protests have been less about poor salaries or the obvious overloading of their time than about what they see as a sustained governmental assault on their autonomy and professionalism, the denigrating of practical experience and educational research. The Dearing Report (1993)

9 The complex story is vividly told in Stuart Maclure, *The Inspectors' Calling: HMI and the Shaping of Educational Policy 1945–1992*, 2001.

clearly recognised the validity of teachers' complaints but did little to allay teachers' fears that they were being reduced to operatives who delivered someone else's curriculum. That curriculum is now delivered to schools in piles of beautifully presented papers and ring binders, each laying down the aims and objectives of the programme at particular stages, with lesson outlines, tasks, worksheets, homework and assessment. The nationwide standardising process might have been thought to diminish the amount of paper; in fact, it has increased it. One recent research work describes the change in teachers' situations like this:

> From being perceived—and perceiving themselves—as central players in the grand social engineering project called the welfare state, consulted on its expansion and shape, facilitated by conciliatory management and politics in operating it, they have come to find themselves increasingly marginalised from the policy process, increasingly distrusted by media and the general public, and being invited to provide no more than their technical expertise within managerial strategies and policies devised elsewhere.[10]

It was not surprising, then, that a majority of teachers seem to have joined the rejoicing of other workers in the public sector at the Conservative defeat on 2 May 1997, anticipating major changes in education policy. They had heard Tony Blair proclaim that "education will be a priority for me in government", that with Labour "education will have greater status than ever before," and that Labour would provide "an education system to match the best in the world".[11] But what actually changed after Labour came to power? The emphasis was put on managerial continuity and toughness. Stephen Byers suggested that heads should become more like chief executives of businesses and need not be drawn from the teaching profession at all. David

10 Mike Bottery and Nigel Wright, *Teachers and the State*, 2000, p. 84
11 Tony Blair, Ruskin 20th anniversary lecture, 16 December 1996

Blunkett forecast that teachers would have "to take on the role of learning managers".[12] The education minister Estelle Morris angered teacher unions by telling them that the Labour Party had "learned to like" independent schools, and that state schools had "much to learn" from them.[13] The political judgements to leave the Baker measures in place, to support Chris Woodhead as Chief Inspector with his cohorts of private profit-making firms of inspectors, to step up testing and to increase central control of the curriculum antagonised many Labour-voting teachers. Highly prescriptive directions were given not only about time to be spent but also about teaching methods to be used in improving literacy and numeracy in primary schools. When Lord Baker was asked about Blunkett's measures, he retorted sardonically: "He seems to have recycled a lot of my speeches."

Three years after the election, a survey of 500 teachers' opinions showed that only one in seven believed that the general quality of their jobs had improved during the Labour years, whereas over a half felt that it had got worse. Nine out of ten believed that bureaucracy had grown during that period, and virtually all of them blamed the government for this. The reasons for their dissatisfaction were primarily the heavy work-load and managerial bureaucracy (mentioned by nine out of ten), or stress, rather than pay. The discussions held with focus groups showed that the motives drawing teachers to the profession were vocational: working with children, the pleasures of the classroom, and the sense of a worthwhile job. "But the subject that dominated discussion was all the bureaucracy inflicted by government: administrative paperwork and repeated changes to the syllabus . . . . The secondary teachers who voted Labour in 1997 felt let down. The mention of David Blunkett aroused little enthusiasm. . . . Mention of Chris Woodhead aroused outright antagonism."[14]

12 *The Guardian*, 30 September 2000 13 *Ibid.*, 7 January 2000 14 *Ibid.*, 7 March 2000

The last quarter of a century has irreversibly politicised the management of education. It may be well that teachers and lecturers should have been forced into awareness that they live in a political climate. However, there are dangers for society when the framing of policy abandons the search for consensus in favour of direct political legislation. One result has been to breed a culture of mistrust that devalues the professional, public-service ethic. Government speakers seem unwilling or unable to address the causes of discontent, and sometimes resort to bitterness. Tony Blair talked frustratedly of "the scars on my back" from trying to push through changes in health and education; David Blunkett castigated teacher unions for questioning his decisions. But low-trust, high-control "pushing through" of the government kind is unproductive in education, where the majority of workers are motivated by idealism rather than simple self-interest. As a recent report has concluded, to bring about change through innovation is inevitably risky and demands trust, "something the Government's present management style, all audits, inspections and qualifications, is practically guaranteed to extinguish".[15] The government is blamed for a Soviet-style stick-and-carrot approach. "Things we know didn't work in the private sector—performance-related pay, standards, budgetary management and the like—are strangling the public sector. Public sector organisations are over-managed . . . ."[16] Even a task force set up by Tony Blair found, according to its chairman, that the D/EE was "the most Stalinist department I have ever come across".[17] The excuse for introducing new bureaucratic control methods

15 Public Management Foundation, *Wasted Values: Harnessing the Commitment of Public Managers*, 1999

16 Simon Caulkin, "All Mouth and Standards", *The Observer*, 31 October 1999

17 *The Guardian*, 5 April 2000. The government's policy seems to embody Douglas McGregor's Theory X of worker management, which assumes that people are immature, lazy, incapable of managing themselves, and have to be driven by carrot and stick. By contrast, Theory Y assumes that people are adults who find satisfaction in work and want achievement and responsibility.

to ensure "accountability" is always that (in the view of the managers and administrators) the workers' competence or performance is in doubt (hence Woodhead's notorious harping on "failing" teachers). If there is resistance, then sanctions must be brought in against some to divide the labour force (hence the league tables, lists of failing schools, awards for superior teachers). In order to eliminate "discrepancies", methods must be found to establish standardised patterns and routines (hence the national curriculum and the associated testing, and compulsory "initiatives" like the literacy hour). The administration increasingly tries to control individual varieties of behaviour through rules and prescribed objectives (hence the stress on "competences" which new teachers have to display, and the use of OFSTED reports to establish set models of "best practice"). It is a return to the world of Gradgrind and M'Choakumchild. Mike Bottery has suggested that this is the central dilemma facing all bureaucracies,

> and particularly public services, such as education, which are peopled by human beings who must deal with other human beings. This treatment ideally should be carried out on an individual caring basis, through the discretion of the practitioner. Yet in reality the service is delivered through a form of organization geared to mass treatment, detachment, equal service and consistency. . . . The bureaucratic organization, by its very design, then, prohibits and contradicts one of the ultimate aims of its practitioners. . . . This tension between individual and organization is heightened the more that the organization attempts to place accountability controls upon its members.[18]

The continual political stress on teachers' *accountability* narrows the meaning of that concept to the formal contract: the teachers' legal and political responsibility

---

18 Mike Bottery, *The Ethics of Educational Management*, 1992, pp. 44–5

towards the authorities (claiming to represent some abstract "public") that employ them. It deliberately discounts other significant forms of accountability: the *professional* responsibility that teachers feel towards their role and their relationship with other teachers, their *moral* accountability towards individual pupils and their needs, and their responsibility towards their *subject*, with its academic demands and specific disciplinary teaching styles. The conflict between these different account-abilities underlies much of the mutual suspicion between managers (politicians and administrators) on the one hand and practitioners (teachers and researchers) on the other.

Let us be clear about this. We are not suggesting that the government should not have firm views on education, or that the minister and others are not well-intentioned. Our concern is twofold. First, Conservative and Labour parties have been prodigal with "initiatives" in education but without giving any sense of a coherently developing *policy* for the service. Second, the decisions that are taken use all the techniques of modern managerialism to overcome resistance from those who have to implement the measures and to compel their compliance. Deliberately or not, the subtext beneath the rhetoric is almost always that teachers are untrustworthy, that they will abuse autonomy, that they can only be motivated by sticks or carrots. We could parade all too many examples where a central "firm persuasion" has turned out to be dubious or simply wrong. The government's bravely launched Key Skills programme, according to the first research evaluation, is "a disaster", unpopular with students and staff and ignored by employers and universities.[19] Consider, as one typical example, the government's determination to introduce pay

19 Nuffield Foundation study, reported in *The Guardian*, 20 March, 2001. Members of the National Association of Head Teachers, meeting in May 2001, described the new sixth form curriculum as a "shambles" and claimed that most schools would boycott the key-skills tests in future.

differentials in the profession to reward "good" teachers. A large-scale "consultation process" was carried out, but when the results showed that considerably more teachers were opposed than in favour, the D/EE simply ignored them. The new system that a majority of teachers resisted was announced in threadbare terms that repeated "management" like a mantra and relied a good deal on faith rather than specifics: "Performance management is central to our proposals and offers significant benefits to schools" (*such as?*); "Our proposals entail a significant strengthening of performance management in schools" (*why?*); "Performance management should help teachers improve their own effectiveness" (*how?*). In place of justification, readers were offered very clear details about how the scheme would be managed. "We have been developing a draft Performance Management Framework which will set out the key elements of the new system." First there would be "draft guidelines on the new performance management system"; a training day would be "designated for work on performance management"; then "appraisal regulations underpinning effective new systems of performance management would take statutory effect." The shift from bland assertions of helping, through guiding, to regulation and then statutory obligation, is a standard management sequence. As we are rightly told that the system would depend on "soundly-based evidence of effective teaching", it might be expected that help would be sought from those who know most about good teaching. Not a bit of it: "We have commissioned research from management consultants Hay McBer to help set those standards."

The lack of awareness of professional feeling—or the determination to ignore it—has been neatly illustrated as we write by two "major" policy statements. The first of these outlined the plans—typically, first revealed to the press rather than to the profession—for what was called a "major shake-up for state schools". The product of yet another new policy and management department within the D/EE, this "shake-up" involves wide-ranging plans to scrap the traditional school day, to teach children in different institutions rather than in one school, to introduce new "independent" state schools with private money, and to control the secondary curriculum even more tightly (with literacy, numeracy and science hours "under strict guidance from Whitehall"). The changes, we were told, would be implemented within three months, despite angry protests from teachers and local government. This is the new brutal face of management in education. Policy is driven by concern for how it will "play" in the media, not by consultation with those who have to implement it. So *Beacon Schools* were launched in 1998 to be "a guiding light for others to follow", followed in September 2000 by the announcement of a thousand new *specialist* schools in Arts, Language and Technology to be "hotbeds of talent", and then the intention to increase these to "at least" 1,500 schools by the year 2006. Such heavily puffed initiatives have been seen by many teachers as increasing selection and destroying the model of a planned, local, integrated education service based on the principles of comprehensive education. It is hard to see why specialist schools should be so appealing to a Labour administration: "diversity is not a strategy but a cop-out."[20]

The second example has been the launch of *Active Citizenship*, a two-hundred-page booklet preparing for this to become yet another compulsory item to be crammed into the 11–16 curriculum from September 2002. Those of us

20 The plans were originally revealed to the press and reported, for example, in *The Observer*, 11 June 2000. Since then there has been a "sustained attack" on the proposals by different teacher groups, notably the Secondary Heads' Association, whose general secretary said that members had "expressed amazement" and were "deeply concerned" at this "failure to support the principle of the comprehensive school" (*The Guardian*, 24 May 2001). The final phrase is quoted from Professor Alan Smithers, who wrote in the same issue of *The Guardian* under the headline "Labour creating Secondary Maze".

who taught English, history, religion or other subjects may well have believed that we were already dealing with citizenship in terms of particular, specific examples. To separate out Citizenship as a subject in itself implies both that we were mistaken and that our political managers know better. The simplistic proposals behind the American-inspired booklet seem to imagine that those trained in citizenship will participate more fully in "the democratic process". We are being asked to take on trust that the role-playing, writing of mission-statements, learning to spell "key Citizenship words" will achieve something of value, perhaps even the "self-empowerment" that is talked about. As one critic responded to the language of the booklet, she felt as we do that the examples "bear a close resemblance to the type of activities in which management consultants indulge on training weekends away in the Welsh hills."[21] Among the different concerns of the new curriculum, one is to ensure that children leave school better equipped to manage their personal finances and make choices as "informed consumers". It is hardly surprising that this is the one element that has been greeted with enthusiasm outside the schools. Financial organisations are already busy producing classroom resources for teachers and contributing funds to the Personal Finance Education Group. They include Pro-Share, the organisation which promotes share ownership, the Financial Services Authority, Britannic Assurance, and the NatWest Financial Literacy Centre for Education & Industry at the University of Warwick.

Underlying these and many other examples of managerial determination is the resentment that so many politicians show for "professors of education" and for educational research. This dislike can be explained (though not excused) on two main grounds. First, there is the discrepancy of time scales. Respectable educational research, especially if it involves longitudinal studies of

21 Dea Birkett, "Are you a Good Citizen?", *The Guardian*, 12 December 2000

students, extends over years. By contrast, politicians work on a short time-scale: they want answers yesterday and cannot wait because their eyes are always fixed on the next election. Changes are seen as important because they can be presented to make it look as though government is actually achieving something. Second, there is a discrepancy between truth and expediency. Politicians like research that seems to support what they want to do, and they ignore or disparage uncomfortable findings. The *Guardian* interview with Kenneth Baker quoted above made plain that he was well aware that his measures rested on no firm research, but only on ideological conviction. One might have thought that his new system

> would have to be built on a particularly strong intellectual foundation, a great deal of solid research and clear thinking. Not so. The most sweeping educational reforms this century, it transpires, had just as much to do with guesswork, personal whim and bare-knuckle politics. . . . And this whole shift was achieved with barely a fact behind it. Politically, it was brilliant. Educationally, it was a hoax. . . . The politics of education are built on foundations of ignorance.

In their desire to raise standards, politicians of all parties prefer instant ideology and the quick fix to the long struggle for understanding. Much (possibly orchestrated) media publicity has been given to official sneers at educational research and to government criticisms of research projects when the findings apparently contradict current policy. For example, when David Blunkett suggested that schools (especially at primary level) should be setting more homework for their pupils, his announcement happened to coincide with the publication of a report appearing to show that those who claimed to do the most homework were not the pupils with the highest test scores.[22] The then

22 S. J. Farrow, P. B. Tymms and B. Henderson, "Homework and Attainment in Primary Schools", *British Educational Research Journal*, 25 (3), pp. 323–41

Secretary of State's reaction was to make a violent attack on the researchers who, he said, were "so out of touch with reality that they churn out findings which no-one with the slightest common sense could take seriously."[23] Blunkett's mind was already made up; he was unwilling to consider anything that suggested that his advice might be unhelpful. As the researchers commented: "In the long run it would seem that educational research is doomed to attract a bad press and public denigration by politicians. Any work that generates unexpected results runs the risk of being rubbished."[24]

At the other extreme, the government is all too anxious to promote (and pay for) research that will support its own policies. It has been swift to invest heavily in educational computing, committing a billion pounds for establishing a "National Grid for Learning" by 2002, greatly increasing supplies of educational hardware and software, and taking steps to ensure nationwide schools' connection to the Internet. These decisions and this expenditure have been justified on grounds of the presumed educational benefit. A glowing press release said that the National Grid for Learning "has enormous potential for improving attainment, for supporting our main goal of driving up standards in schools and for delivering material which is of immediate, practical and working use to schools."[25] However, even those working in that field are conscious that there is little, if any, evidence that the use of information technology in education will necessarily lead to any educational improvements.[26] A hidden agenda for

23 David Blunkett addressing the CBI on 19 July 1999

24 British Educational Research Association, *Research Intelligence* No. 70, December 1999

25 DfEE Press Release 184/98

26 For example, the Chief Executive of the British Agency for Education Communications and Technology has expressed concern at "the fragility of the evidence base linking ICT use with improvements in teaching and learning" (Keynote Speech, BETT 99, 14 January 1999). Also see N. Selwyn, "Why the Computer Is Not Dominating Schools: a Failure of Policy or a Failure of Practice?" *Cambridge Journal of Education*, 29(1), 1999, pp. 77–91.

research and practice is being driven by an official concern to prove that educational technology does "work". The way in which policy-makers assume results that researchers and teachers will then be expected to deliver (common in totalitarian states) is shown in press releases like this:

> With Government strategy now requiring ICT to be fundamental to the effectiveness of schools in the future, the task for educationalists is to ensure that the National Grid for Learning becomes a powerful vehicle for improving standards.[27]

The reason for ICT to be fundamental to school effectiveness is not an educational one but a *requirement* of government strategy. There is no need to await research showing how far the National Grid for Learning actually improves standards; it is an imposed *task* for educationalists to *ensure* that it does.

The wider results of this managerial obsession with controlling all aspects of teaching and research are plain. What has happened to the sense of vocation and to the public esteem in which teachers are held? Fewer and fewer young people choose teaching as a career, despite expensive advertising campaigns ("nobody forgets a good teacher"; "those who can, teach"). Over the years, the drop in the number of applications for undergraduate teacher training courses contrasts with the steady rise in the number of students wanting to undertake courses in marketing. Numbers are now being further reduced by the new compulsory maths tests for trainee teachers, which have almost universally been greeted as "madness", "bungled", "patronising and insulting".[28] Because of chronic staff

27 National Council for Educational Technology, Press Release, Coventry, 7 October 1997

28 *The Guardian*, 19 May, 2001. With typical managerial conceit, a spokesman for the DfEE claimed all the merit for improving teaching standards, while apparently being unaware that "training colleges" had gone out of existence years ago. He said: "We make absolutely no apology whatsoever for reforming our teacher training colleges. They failed to teach teachers properly for several decades until we introduced the first training curriculum."

shortages, the government introduces measures to recruit unqualified "classroom assistants" and to make it easier to poach teachers from overseas countries to fill the gaps. More than three-quarters of schoolchildren, and nine out of ten boys, have ruled out any thoughts of a career in teaching by the time they are sixteen.[29] Meanwhile many of those actually teaching would prefer to leave. Inspections cause stress, absenteeism and even suicide ("OFSTED screws people up," says an NUT official). A sixth of all teachers complain of being bullied by managers recently[30] and increasing numbers are suing their authorities after being assaulted by pupils.[31] Half of the total teaching force expects to have left the profession within ten years. Even among those under 35, more than a third expect to have abandoned teaching by that time.[32] In the Conservative years teachers (and particularly experienced senior teachers) queued up to leave the profession to which they had devoted their working lives. The escape route via early retirement proved so popular that it had to be closed off by the government in 1997. Apparently millions of pounds have since been set aside to recompense those who—in government-speak—"are not able to carry forward the changes envisaged in improving education." Simultaneously more sums are earmarked to pay for a force of external advisers and assessors to judge how effectively existing heads are "carrying forward the changes", and to assess which teachers should be handed extra performance-related pay.[33] Despite an increase in salary levels, vacancies for head teachers have reached record levels. In schools (and increasingly in colleges and universities) there is bitter dissatisfaction with the way in which education is being managed, from the top and lower down. As one successful

29 *The Times*, 9 April 2000
30 *The Observer*, 2 April 2000 and 23 April 2000
31 *The Times*, 12 April 2000
32 *The Guardian*, 29 February 2000
33 "Jaded Heads will be Paid Off", *The Times Educational Supplement*, 12 November 1999

teacher said on being driven out after thirty years, "There is no freedom any more. It's gone. Initiative and resourcefulness are banned. Every school has become part of the gulag."[34] Why should anyone wish to belong to a profession that is over-controlled, over-worked, under-valued and simultaneously blamed for so many of society's problems?

34 Bob Hewitt, reported in *The Guardian*, 9 January 2001

7

Managing the Deity

For centuries in Britain cultural debate constantly invoked
Christian values, but in an increasingly secular age that is
no longer true. The theologian Don Cupitt speaks for many
when he says that the "great cultural event" dominating his
life has been "the collapse of religious meaning that has
been taking place since the end of World War II", which
he calls "perhaps the most severe and sudden cultural rupture
in the whole of human history".[1] For many people,
meaning is no longer given to everyday life by the
churches, by the language of Bible and prayer-book, but by
the modes and cultural assumptions adopted by the
powerful economic and political movements of the last
century: *laissez-faire* Capitalism, Marxism, State Socialism
and the rather shadowy "Third Way". We have argued that
the most insidiously powerful of these is the modern
obsession with managerialism, which derives much of its
power from subtly trading in the language of both political
and religious systems.

   Modern management impinges directly on Christianity
in two obvious ways. First, because it marginalises and
downgrades cultural history, it inevitably denies the importance of Christian traditions, to the alarm of agnostics as
well as Christians. Journalists like Polly Toynbee demand
rhetorically, "How can people look at a painting or

1 Don Cupitt, *After God*, 1997, pp. vii, ix

sculpture or read a book of previous centuries or understand anything about history if they don't know this most essential Christian story?"[2] Second, by replacing the moral codes of Christian belief with its own mechanistic imperatives, management sees the church itself not as a distinct faith-community but as simply another secular organisation to be "managed" in essentially the same way as an industry, a political party or a supporters club. The extent to which this thinking has infected the churches is illustrated by the news (January 2001) that Church of England clergy are to petition the government to alter their legal status, so that they are seen as employees of the church rather than of God.

There are many levels on which managerial thinking is coming to dominate life within the Christian churches, and other ways in which management is cynically making use of the churches' residual powers. In this chapter we shall examine two questions in particular. First, what kind of impact are the styles of modern management in industry and in politics having on the churches, as they struggle to respond to shrinking membership and belief? Second, at the domestic level, how should the churches themselves, as institutions, be administered and managed?

The Christian churches understandably lack self-confidence in the face of dwindling membership (now down to something like 7.5% of the population), financial problems, and increasing hostility from a predominantly secular society. There have been dramatic prognostications of the "Death of God": that the church "is spiralling towards an apparent death,"[3] or "will be dead in forty years time," when "all claims that Britain is a Christian nation will finally have to be given up."[4] The number of members in the Methodist church has roughly halved since the time in the

2 Polly Toynbee, "Our Lost Religion", *The Guardian*, 13 April, 2001

3 Jack Spong, "The Church is Dead, Long Live the Reformation", *The Guardian*, 9 December 2000

4 Hazel Southam in *The Independent*, 16 April 2000, citing an analysis by Peter Brierley

early nineteen-thirties when three separate groups united in one. In the last decade, it has been reckoned that membership of the Anglican church has dropped by 40% and that of the Roman Catholics by 35%. Nearly 400 priests left the Church of England during the dispute over women's ordination. It has been plausibly suggested that there may now be more practising Muslims than Christians in Britain. One response to this has been a typically managerial call to massage the figures by redefining what membership means and who should be counted. Another has been to increase demands for better "promotion" of religion (once called *mission* and now termed *outreach*). Such efforts have had little or no effect and, at the beginning of a new Millennium, a leading evangelist has said that he was "deeply disappointed" that the Decade of Evangelism, which he helped to launch in January 1991, had been a "complete failure".[5] Falling membership is accompanied by dwindling belief. According to recent surveys, only a quarter of those questioned had any belief in a personal God, only just over half knew what Easter celebrates, and only half of those under 25 believed that Jesus actually lived.[6]

Increasingly strident cries are being made to remedy this situation by better management and marketing, copied from the business world. Some point hopefully to the success of the *Alpha* courses, where slick videos, youthful enthusiasts and well-mounted dinner parties put a gloss on somewhat conservative theology. Suggesting that "the Church of England is now competing for customers in a market place", one paper on the Web demands "Why has the Church not embraced marketing management as the basis of its missionary strategy?" Such enthusiasm for "marketing" religion like soap-powder assumes a hierarchical power structure in which "experts" make decisions,

5 *The Methodist Recorder*, 16 December 1999. In fact, it has been reckoned that during the Decade of Evangelism church attendance actually fell by over 20%.

6 Opinion Research Business enquiries in conjunction with *The Tablet*, April 2000 and 2001

and lower groups carry them out as ordered. How does this fit with views of the church as generally a voluntary society, organised in local churches? The expectations that more efficient presentation and "modern" methods will significantly attract members to the church have too often been shown as quite unreal.

For a long period the church *has* gingerly been trying to promote itself more widely. In a play for "relevance" and popularity, the Bible was reissued in modern, more conversational prose (*The Good News Bible*), which also succeeded in alienating many traditional supporters. John Robinson attempted a modest demythologising of religion in terms of current psychology and sociology in his popular *Honest to God* (1963). There were attempts to harness new youth-friendly evangelical movements from North America, bringing pop-star missioners to mass meetings and using the resources of cinema, radio and television. Later there would be even more desperate attempts to get "back in touch"—vicars in mufti, new clap-happy forms of church worship with dancing and strobe lights, pop stars preaching, priests doubling as stand-up comedians, banal worship songs and services devoted to the celebration of the motor car, gay love or domestic pets, whatever might bring people in. The Church of England hastened to shed its exclusively male image, pressing ahead (as the Methodists had done) with the ordination of women priests. The Roman Catholic Church abandoned the Latin Mass in favour of the vernacular, the Anglicans largely ditched the *Book of Common Prayer* for more user-friendly liturgies, culminating in the publication of *Common Worship* in Autumn 2000,[7] and the Methodists purged their new orders of service to eliminate "sexist" language (offending some by one prayer that addressed God as Mother). Like a chain of failing department stores, the churches seemed to be rushing to change

---

7 For some lively comments on this process, see Peter Mullen (ed.), *The Real Common Worship*, Denton, 2000.

their image before their market share evaporated altogether. However, none of these attempts to "appeal" seems to have succeeded.

The facts of decline in the institutional churches do not, of course, mean that secularism has eliminated religion as such. In the surveys previously cited, only 8% of the population described themselves as atheists. The fastest growing cults today are not those that insist on adherence to church discipline, but the freer Pentecostal and so-called "cafeteria" or do-it-yourself groups, that claim to "take the best and leave the rest" of older religions. The result has been a strange, segmented mix of "niche" church groups: the Moonies, the Jesus Army, the Christian Coalition, Bikers for Jesus, the Toronto Blessing, Scientologists, Eco-Spiritualists, Sea of Faith, the Aetherious Society, the Unification Church, Spring Harvest. Media evangelists head huge commercial operations and advertise their power to perform "miracles". More widely, astrology and the occult seem at least as popular as ever, with those interested in witchcraft now actually seeking publicity rather than secrecy. Gaia and other Green semi-religions claim increasing membership. In their different ways, all these can be read as affirmations that faith continues, but also that it belongs in the private or individual sphere. According to the surveys cited, nearly 40% of people claim to have received answers to their prayers, but most of them prefer to describe themselves as "spiritual" rather than "religious". Residual belief there clearly is, but largely of a non-institutional kind that rejects the claims of the churches to organise the life and behaviour of individuals.

In a managerialist state, it is almost inevitable that decline will be blamed on defective organisation, and improvement will be sought through better management and structures *within* the church. This at least seems to offer the possibility of controlling events, when so much else is sliding away. If you see the church primarily as an administrative structure (with thousands of buildings, armies of employees, a hierarchy of offices, enormous financial budgets, a set of laws, a tradition of government and mountains of paper) then you may see salvation in changing that structure, patching up the old wine-skins. Clearly no Christian would suggest that the church should be *inefficiently* run, but surely the machinery is—at best— secondary. The action of God is far wider than his church, which exists not for itself but for God and for those outside it. That action must be organised, but not rigidly structured and packaged on the pattern of a multi-national company. There were unreal dreams in the nineteen-seventies that "The new philosophy of scientific management must help to bring about the Christian philosophy of love and welfare among all nations."[8] Despite the manifest inability of "scientific management" to achieve even much more modest goals, many church leaders have been encouraged to believe in and to promote its mystique. The inevitable result is to reposition the church still further within the cultural sphere of business and government, accepting the expedient values built into their language. Back in 1983 the new Archbishop of York, John Habgood, remarked presciently that "Churches in decline seem to multiply bureaucracies. The weaker the local base on which everything rests, the more pervasive and dominatingly efficient seems the central machinery."[9] There has been a proliferation of organisational reports and discussion papers, with titles like *Challenges for the Church in the Twenty-first Century*.[10]

In a recent article, Mark Chater recorded:

8 N. P. Mouzelis, *Organization and Bureaucracy: An analysis of modern theories*, revised, 1975, p. 84
9 John Habgood, *Church and Nation in a Secular Age*, 1983, p. 113

10 J. S. Freeman, *Challenges for the Church in the Twenty-first Century*, Cowley, 1994. Similar titles might include: *The Christian Message in a Non-Christian World, Refounding the Church, The New Era In Religious Communication, Beyond Belief: Religion in a Post-Traditional World, Re-imagining the Parish, Church and World in the Third Millennium, The Parish in Transition, The Church as Culture in a Post-Christian Society, The Church between Gospel and Culture, The Paradox of the Church in the Postmodern World, Shape of the Church to Come*, or *New Wine-skins: Re-Imagining Religious Life Today*.

The last ten years have seen the churches taking an increasing interest in management. A flurry of books on leadership has accompanied the emergence of courses and associations focusing on the application of management principles and techniques to ecclesiastical contexts [assuming] that any learning from the dialogue will be on the part of the churches, with management as the leader.[11]

This seems to us quite a moderate view of the situation. A quick glance at books currently published for churches comes up with these titles (and there are many more of the same): *Accountable Leadership: A Resource Guide*; *Advanced Strategic Planning : A New Model*; *Basic Budgeting for Churches*; *Business Management in the Local Church*; *Church Administration: Effective Leadership for Ministry*; *Church Administration Handbook*; *Church Staff Handbook: How to Build an Effective Ministry Team*; *Church Office Handbook for Ministers*; *Effective Church Finances: Fund-Raising and Budgeting for Church Leaders*; *The Hands-on Parish*—and our own particular favourite, *101 Things to Do With a Dull Church*. Inevitably the books are accompanied by a growing pile of different software packages for computerised church management, offering— to take one example—a way to "Track Membership, Attendance, Prospects and Finances with ease", a system that is "Powerful, easy to use and network capable, developed from years of church and pastoral experience. Your work will now be easier and more organised. You will be able to do things more quickly and with much more efficiency." This is the new industrial concept of managerialism, for which "effective" and "efficient" are the ultimate accolade. But in the church efficiency is measured by the extent to which God's will is done. Worship, pastoral care, mission and service can never be neatly quantified and cost-efficient in the style of manufacturing industry. Nevertheless, following the pattern of courses in Arts or Sport

11 Mark Chater, "Theology and Management" in *Modern Believing* 40:4 (October 1999) p. 64

Management, a new Master of Business Administration (MBA) course specifically designed for church management was launched in September 1998 at Bishop Grosseteste University College, Lincoln, a Church of England College, in association with the School of Management at Hull University. Details of the course claimed that it had been "developed as a response to perceived management and organisational needs in the Church of England and other Christian communions".

Recent managerial changes in the major protestant churches of England have shifted the focus from the serving role of the church towards the administrative; moving power increasingly away from the members towards the paid employees at the centre. In the Church of England, powers that were previously vested in the (elected) General Synod or the Church Commissioners have been shifted to the new, small Archbishops' Council (whose members are appointed). A "communications department" with its own spin doctors attempts to control what the public should hear. Not everyone has accepted the Council's claim that clarity and coherence necessarily demand central control and a uniform message.[12] Similarly in Methodism, the Faith and Order Committee Report (1999) was a self-examination of the structure, identity and purpose of the church. It resulted in the abolition of existing structures and the appointment of a new controlling central executive (the Methodist Council) with Coordinating Secretaries to move forward a new-look (somewhat Blairite) administration. Some churchgoers have written bitterly of the "crisis of trust" arising when local churches and their pastors feel estranged from an apparently remote decision-making "cabinet" and resent the financial demands being placed upon them.[13]

As we argue throughout this book, adopting the langu-

12 See Monica Furlong, *C of E: The State it's in*, 2000.
13 See, for example, an article by a former president of the Methodist Conference, the Rev. Dr John Vincent in *The Methodist Recorder*, 22 June 2000.

age of modern management inevitably involves taking on the values and priorities that are built into it. In the church as in other organisations we are beginning to see how managerial bureaucracy is gradually reshaping traditional purposes and functions. The Cathedral Measures of 1999 framed in managerial jargon a new set of arrangements for their governance, requiring each to have an Administrator and a new committee to advise on "financial and invest-ment management". It was no surprise that Synod felt that the cathedrals should "protect their image" with a distinctive "trademark". There has been a steady growth in size and complexity of the Standing Orders of the Church of England's General Synod, paralleled by the Methodist Church's CPD (Constitution, Practice and Discipline of the Methodist Church). Centralised bureaucracy has diminished the auto-nomy of parishes or congregations and come to dominate choices that have to be made about church policy, forms of worship and liturgy, the closing and opening of churches, forms of ecumenism, lay and ministerial training, and—of course—financial contributions.

Such self-obsessed management of an inappropriate kind can be seen in the churches' relationship with radio and television. We might expect some considered vision of the future of religious broadcasting, and a critical response to the values of current programming, to the implications of satellite and cable TV and the growth of "niche" channels. But instead of this, the institutional churches react like political parties or multinational companies, narrowly concerned with their image and market share-the amount of time and the timetable placing afforded to specifically religious programmes. One reviewer for the religious press asserted recently that "Anyone who watches television must be aware that over the past ten years the BBC has marginalised religion to the point of extinction."[14] What he meant, of course, was not "religion" as such, but the

14 Rev. David Bridge, *The Methodist Recorder*, 30 November 2000

organised presentation of it sanctified by the churches, living in a sort of cultural ghetto. It does not include or attempt to analyse the influence (for good or bad) of programmes like *Ballykissangel* or *The Vicar of Dibley*. Early in the year 2000 the General Synod of the Church of England received an influential report written by a former BBC producer, *Losing Faith in the BBC*, and debated a well-supported motion calling on the BBC to broadcast more peak-time religious programmes and to "restore the hours of religious television to the average of the 1980s". The Methodist Conference similarly considered a motion urging the BBC to reconsider "the evident marginalisation of religious programmes", urging the clock to be put back. Within the year, the head of the BBC's religious broadcasting unit, the Rev. Ernie Rea, had retired, allegedly in protest at the downgrading of coverage. Ironically, while all this backward-looking bickering had been going on, ITV was lobbying for the elimination of the existing requirement to screen any religious programmes at all.

Further evidence of the way that the churches are seeking to structure themselves along the lines of hierarchical, multi-national companies and corporations can be drawn from the terminology in which they advertise for a new brand of business executives. Significantly, in the creation of the new central executive for Methodism, a senior post responsible for the church's Mission was quietly dropped. Instead, the new senior management team included a Secretary for Political and Parliamentary Affairs and a Secretary for Business and Economic Affairs at salaries well over £30,000 each (strikingly different from the rates at which "ordinary" Methodist ministers are paid). The terms in which the latter post was advertised were significant. A successful candidate would be a person "experienced at management or senior level in business, industry or commerce or experienced in industrial chaplaincy", one who would be "innovative, clear thinking and willing to take risks" and "confident with the media". It would be all too easy to duplicate examples, like the advertisement for a Church Administrator for whom the only requirements are "to be computer literate and enjoy contact with people". Little has yet been done to consider what sort of relationship will exist between this new breed of professional managers and the professional clergy with whom they will be working. Will it matter, for example, that psychologists find that students in business schools show high levels of aggression, contrasted with those in theological training?[15] Will there be particular problems in the Free Churches where all ministers are paid on the same (low) salary scale when managers are offered more than twice as much?

In financial matters, the adoption of modern managerial techniques, with increasing central control, has not proved much of a success. In the Anglican church there was widespread alarm at the failing policies of the church commissioners, who lost at least five hundred million pounds in the early nineteen-nineties through unwise property speculation. More recently, a report for the General Synod in February 2000 suggested that, because of "a cash-flow crisis" the Church of England may have to seek corporate sponsorship for students training to become clergy or try to attract wealthy candidates (possibly from abroad) who will be able to pay their own way through training. More basically, the report warns that the church will have to make managerial decisions about the number of clergy required in terms of projections, rather than (as at present) simply assuming that money will be found to support all those called to ordination.[16] As we write, the Methodist press is full of complaining letters about a shortfall of £1.7 million in the church's finances, and details of ways in which the church is cutting two million pounds from its expenditure by closing activities and looking for support

15 Donald G. Jones, ed., *Business, Religion and Ethics*, Cambridge, Mass., 1982, p. 125
16 *The Guardian* 15 February 2000

from "funding partners". A report of the Methodist Council suggests blandly that "circuits and Districts have not appreciated the huge change that has come over Connexional work and finances since restructuring three years ago", which established "a costed development plan which covers every aspect of Connexional work".[17] How can it be that the obsession with centralised bureaucracy seems to result in less efficient outcomes and heavier demands on local churches? As John Habgood wrote, it is natural for members to wonder why an increasing proportion of their income seems to go in the support of unproductive bureaucrats.[18]

In a modern managerial society, where functions have become separated and specialised, what are the clergy *for*? The clergyman of the eighteenth and nineteenth centuries was typically not only a minister and worship leader but a teacher, a politician, a clerk, a health visitor, an exponent of the law, an agent of charity, having a range of different contacts with the ordinary daily life of his parish. Today, when many of these roles have been taken over by other agencies, he (or she) runs the risk of becoming little more than an administrator of other people and activities. It might be thought that the increasing use of the professional and administrative skills of the churches' lay members (and in the USA the employment of full-time lay administrators) would decrease the administrative burden; instead—as in hospitals and universities—it seems to have increased it. In the United States, where training for the ministry involves management and organisation as an essential part, research suggests that, although ministers rated their administrative role as the least important and least enjoyable part of their work, it was the responsibility on which they had to spend most time, and that very much against their will.[19] The

17 *The Methodist Recorder*, 16 December 1999

18 John Habgood, *op. cit.*, p. 114

19 Donald G . Jones, (ed.), *Business, Religion and Ethics*, Cambridge, Mass., 1982, citing the conclusions of S. Blizzard, 1956; J. H. Stewart, 1969; D. T. Hall and B. Schneider, 1973

cleric has become increasingly pigeonholed in maintaining what are now seen as minority interests—worship and pastoral visiting—and in managing a local church or churches within an imposed structure. In such times of change, clergy become more conscious of their shifting roles, and are forced to compare their own views of ministry with the expectations of their parishioners. They become increasingly aware of the tensions between their vocation and their bureaucratic responsibilities, manifested in their relationship with central administration. "The religious functionary has become increasingly involved in administrative and organisational duties within the context of an ever-growing ecclesiastical bureaucracy."[20]

These problems for the clergy were already plain in the nineteen-sixties. One scholar wrote in 1968 of the churches' attempts to cope with the difficulties of urban areas, where a sense of community had often vanished:

> The main structural response of the Church centrally and locally has been to sub-divide its activities, to correspond to the specialised interests and needs of its members. This increases the functions of co-ordination and supervision, and of administration generally. The clergyman as administrator and co-ordinator of diverse activities and personnel is contrasted in the minds of both clergy and parishioners with the traditional image of the shepherd and his small flock. . . . Not only is there role conflict, which affects the relations between the clergy and central administration, but there is also severe status insecurity.[21]

The warning was clear, but nobody seems to have been listening.

---

20 Stewart Ranson, Alan Bryman and Bob Hinings, *Clergy, Ministers and Priests*, 1977, p. 6
21 Kenneth A. Thompson, *Bureaucracy and Church Reform*, Oxford, 1970, p. 231

8

Rebranding Britain

Having suggested some of the particular ways in which modern management may be harming, even destroying, what it purports to manage, we now turn to the broader question of how Britain is currently "managing", and inevitably harming, *itself*. For it is a basic tenet of this book that Britain generally stands in need not so much of different or "better" management, but of a great deal less of it. Of course this is not the managerialists' view. They would like to see modern managers given even more power, and managerialism functioning within a wholly unquestioning, wholly supportive, "New Britain":

> Organisations that work, like the British army, the Swiss rail system or any German manufacturer, have a powerful culture and ethos that has been built up over time. Their members know what is expected of them, know that the organisation will reward them for doing it well and are proud of what it stands for. Modernisation is inbuilt into the organisation's fabric because everybody has a stake in the future.
>
> Britain's problem is simply stated—with one or two exceptions, we don't provide the context in which our organisations can be led even to reach this point. Our ministers are not leaders of departments of state; they are not in place long enough for that, nor do they define their role in those terms . . . the truth remains, to be other than second rate, we must be

better organised, a proposition as distant as trains that run on time.[1]

"Better organised" usually means more comprehensively managed, with stronger control by the forces of modern managerialism. As this cannot be achieved by state managers alone, we have in recent years been told that "the whole nation" must team up, and enter into "partnership" with the government, to form the ultimate "cultural industry". The necessary "rebranding" of Britain, in the Prime Minister's terms, involves each of us putting our shoulders to the same wheel:

> There is a role for Government, for teamwork and partnership. But it must be a role for today's world. Not about picking winners, state subsidies, heavy regulation; but about education, infrastructure, promoting investment, helping small business and entrepreneurs and fair-ness. To make Britain more competitive, better at generating wealth, but do it on a basis that serves the needs of the whole nation—one nation. This is a policy that is unashamedly long-termist. Competing on quality can't be done by Government alone. The whole nation must put its shoulder to the wheel.[2]

The government's avowed aim, mixed in with its desire to make the country commercially competitive, is to "rebrand" Britain—to fundamentally change what it means to be British. As we shall see, in calling for "partnership" the state managers are asking us to deny our cultural history and instead to live by a "national identity" defined by political slogans. We are to become "one nation", but a nation in denial of its own long-established character.

The government's attempted "rebranding" of Britain has three stages: 1) the commodification of every part of life, including not just religion, the arts and education, but hitherto unconsidered entities such as "ambition", "creativity"

1 Will Hutton, "Thank Heavens for Sven", *The Observer*, 8 April 2001
2 Tony Blair, *Speech to CBI*, 27 May 1998

and "fairness"; 2) ceding to the state's managers the right
to measure and pass judgement on all these things—in
matters of "quality"[3] as much as of quantity; and 3)
repackaging these evaluated commodities not just as the
incidental products of the country, but as the *essence* of
New Britain.

It is hard to overstate the enormity of the ambition.
Private life, together with separate public and private sectors,
are all, by command of the modern managers, now driven
by one industrial wheel. British history, unless it can be
packaged and profitably sold on the international market,
is to be ignored, and the British constitution, when it fails
to suit commercial convenience, dismantled. Nothing,
unless it can be measured, packaged and officially marketed
by the new state managers, is now deemed to be of the
slightest importance. This is a cultural change so immense
that the meaning of culture has itself changed out of all
recognition; never before in British history has the common
culture required state sanction and official validation. Only
fifty years ago, as George Orwell pointed out, life in Britain
was essentially compounded of *un*official pleasures:

> We are a nation of flower-lovers, but also a nation of
> stamp-collectors, pigeon-fanciers, amateur carpenters,
> coupon-snippers, darts-players, crossword-puzzle fans.
> All the culture which is most truly native centres around
> things which even when they are communal are not
> official—the pub, the football match, the back garden,
> the fireside and the "nice cup of tea". The liberty of the
> individual is still believed in, almost as in the nineteenth
> century. But this has nothing to do with economic liberty,
> the right to exploit others for profit. It is the liberty to
> have a home of your own, to do what you like in your
> spare time, to choose your own amusements instead of
> having them chosen for you from above.[4]

3 Notice how casually, but with what authority, the Prime Minister drops the term
"quality" in to his CBI speech.
4 George Orwell, "England your England", *Inside the Whale and other Essays*, 1941,
Penguin repr. 1957, p. 66

But now the twin tentacles of "policy-making" and bureaucratic legislation have so infiltrated every part of life that there is hardly a thought or action in modern Britain that is completely, and legitimately, personal or unofficial.

Half a century ago the British mocked the 5- and 10-year plans of the Soviet Union, and were shocked by the way everything human was reduced to statistical comparisons by General Stalin. But now the British "Culture Secretary" can talk of creative activity within his own country in the same grim mechanical terms, without meeting either ridicule or protest:

> If you compare the census figures for 1981 and 1991 . . . there was, on average, a 34% increase in the number of individuals with cultural occupations over the ten-year period. Clothing designers showed an 88% increase; artists and graphic designers a 71% increase; actors, entertainers, producers and directors a 47% increase; and authors, writers and journalists a 43% increase.[5]

Indeed such numbing parades of cultural "fact" are now taken to be some sort of national achievement. In just ten years, the British have got 34% more cultured![6]

At the time of the London Olympics, in 1948, the British still took some pride in being "good sports" as well as good organisers. The horror of the 1936 Berlin Olympics, which Hitler had used as a showcase for his new Reich, was still fresh in many minds. We still abhorred the way in which totalitarian states—such as the Soviet Union—used sport to promote their "national image", and involved the full resources of the state to train their athletes. We took a wry pleasure in the fact that the only British competitor to win a gold medal in the London games was, in fact, a horse.[7]

5 Chris Smith, *Creative Britain*, 1998, p. 10

6 It is obvious, if these extraordinary increases were to be maintained, that by the year 2075 there would in Britain be more clothing designers than people.

7 He was called Foxhunter.

But British sport has now fallen to state managerialism. When Chancellor Gordon Brown announced in his *2000 Annual Spending Review* that he was doubling the existing Treasury funding for British sport, the *Times* correspondent explained:

> The government has become embarrassed by the lack of international success in many activities. . . . Although the money will be handed over to the two quangos for distribution, the Government is keen to see that the money is spent as the department wants, hastening the day when it takes direct control of the funding of British sport.[8]

Increasingly people insisted that the British government must have direct responsibility for every kind of sporting activity. As the Chair of the Regional Sports Board for the South East [*sic*] wrote at the time:

> It is true that parents, clubs and schools must work together and pool resources to develop sporting champions. It is also true that they look to the two great Departments of State [*Department for Education and Employment* and the *Department of Culture, Media and Sport*] to speak and act as one on the question of sport in our national culture, for without the uninamity and the resources to produce more talent and better results we will stay in the doldrums in all our major sports.[9]

Thus "talent", like "quality", is now to be marked out by government for its own promotional use. Whether sporting or artistic, it will play its part in the development of a "New Britain", in which designated talent, nurtured in the quality-controlled cultural industries, will comprehensively "rebrand" Britain, raise its standing overseas and (need you ask) also increase its wealth.

So there was shock in government circles when a 1998 report suggested that after two decades of "modernisation",

8 *The Times*, 19 July 2000
9 Letter to *The Times*, 21 July 2000

"regeneration" and "development", topped up with several months of New Labour government, Britain was of all things still being talked about as an *old country with a long history!* This particularly alarmed the Culture Secretary:

> The recent Demos work is frightening in the evidence it amasses about the way in which as a nation we look backwards . . . the Demos authors dryly tell us: "Around the world . . . Britain's image remains stuck in the past. . . . Britain is seen as a backward-looking has-been, a theme-park world of Royal pageantry and rolling green hills, where draught blows through people's houses."[10]

So naturally Mr Smith and his cabinet colleagues set themselves the task of correcting that misconception—not by supplying households with official draught excluders, but by setting about changing "the national identity". Mr Smith anticipated that results would be almost instantaneous: "I suspect it [*the overseas perception of Britain's modernity*] is changing for the better in a way the Demos work has not yet picked up."[11]

For the government was convinced that not only were such things as university education, religious worship, the arts, dieting, national enterprise levels and British tennis in need of more modern management, so was Britain itself. The relentless application of modern management should be, *must* be, changing the "national identity", must be wiping out the perception of Britain as being an old country, with a long history. The very idea! "The shift we need to make," Peter Mandelson explained, "is from defining ourselves by our past to defining ourselves by our future."[12] "Change", "New Britain", "Today's World", "Moving Forward" and "Competing on Quality" were soon slogans on the lips of every cultural rebrander. Even the Queen's 1999 Christmas Broadcast had modish New Labour soundbites inserted in

10 Chris Smith, *op. cit.*, p. 38   11 *Ibid.*

12 Peter Mandelson, speaking at the Dome's "launch", 3 November 1997

it. "As I look to the future . . . the one certainty is change," recited Her Majesty gloomily, adding that the future offered "opportunity" and (though the statement was belied by her expression) assuring us that all this vacuous drivel was "a source of excitement" to her. And, as ever, in the vanguard of the new futurism was the indomitable Mr Smith:

> We must not define ourselves solely in terms of the past, or tradition, or what we have inherited. Culture and personal and national identity are every bit as much—if not more—about the future, as they are about the past.[13]

Having made this riddling pronouncement Mr Smith and his colleagues set about burying the past. British history was, for example, now virtually excluded from the national school curriculum, except, as Professor Scruton pointed out, "as an occasion for instilling guilt, doubt and repudiation".[14]

Then came the Greenwich Dome—the centrepiece of the government's "Millennium Experience" in the year 2000. Whatever may now be said of that strange enterprise, there is no doubt that it was intended to be both a celebration of modern managerialism, and a monument to the rebranding of Britain. It was intended to define "New Britain" in terms of its future. This was in contrast to the "Festival of Britain" of half a century before. Then, in the words of the official catalogue, the aim had been to celebrate British history, to recreate the collective personality of the British people "from birth to maturity":

> This we shall not do by any system of abstractions, but by letting the work of British men and women, past and present, give evidence of their belief and purpose. It will be the work not of one city but of the whole nation. The Festival will exhibit our standards in the arts and in design, our integrity and imagination in the sciences and in industry, the values—personal and

13 Chris Smith, *op. cit.*, p. 38
14 Roger Scruton, "Don't let Blair ruin it", *The Spectator*, 1 April 2000

collective—which have designed and now operate our society.

The "Millennium Experience", by contrast, appeared to consist of nothing but a system of abstractions. The Dome was to be a triumphal statement of the state managers' desire to commodify, package and market a totally "rebranded" country, a "New Britain" of soundbites and spin that was somehow intended to replace the Britain of history. In 1997, only six months after New Labour had taken office, Peter Mandelson, then Minister without Portfolio and in charge of the millennium celebrations, was unequivocal:

> The Dome will stand as an international testament to our nation's standing—modern, fair and strong—in the contemporary world as well as to the quality of British design and ingenuity.[15]

In a speech in November 1997, Mr Mandelson announced—as a matter of unchallengeable fact—that there would be at least 12 million visitors to the Dome, of whom two million would be tourists. "All of them," he informed us, "will go home with an exciting and enticing story to tell about modern Britain."[16] The Dome would make an essential difference (a "step change" in modern managerial jargon) to the way in which Britain was perceived. His cabinet colleagues added that it was to be the centrepiece of the Labour government's first term in office, and "the first paragraph" of New Labour's next election manifesto.[17] To which rhapsodical stargazing Mr Smith added his own peck of soothsayer's wisdom:

> With the meridian passing through Greenwich, we can really claim that the new millennium starts here. . . . The Millennium Experience at Greenwich, an extraordinary

15 Peter Mandelson, *op. cit.*   16 *Ibid.*
17 The Deputy Prime Minister now denies having said this. He was also reported as saying that if they couldn't manage the Greenwich Dome, they weren't much of a government.

showcase for British talent, a place to educate, to amuse and to amaze, and linked to a nationwide programme of activity, can be used as a draw to visitors who will remember it all their lives. And to those who say, around the country and elsewhere in London, that the Dome will draw visitors away from other attractions, I say: "Think bold." There will be twelve million visitors coming to Greenwich. They will not just want to visit the Dome. We need to ensure that they will want to taste and see the whole range of what Britain as a country has to offer.[18]

However it soon became clear that the projected "outcomes", including the anticipated delight of the Dome's twelve and a half million visitors, were just about the only things which the organisers could agree upon. There was absolutely no agreement about what was actually to be put *in* to the Dome in order to produce this general euphoria. Rumours of inharmonious relations between the 11 designers who had won multi-million pound contracts to design segments of the Dome began to surface. Stephen Bayley, the chief design consultant, who had been advertised as playing the kind of central role that Henry Cole had played in the 1851 Great Exhibition, resigned, complaining of bureaucratic confusion and the "interfering manipulation" of the government spin doctors. Then it was for many months proclaimed that the central arena would witness a lavish musical spectacular produced by Sir Cameron Mackintosh, but, there being no agreement over what this might actually comprise, Sir Cameron faded from the scene. But when in the Spring of 1998 Peter Mandelson surprised the public by paying a visit to Disneyland Paris, the public was reassured that, although it was not yet clear of what it would actually consist, the "Millennium Experience" would be educational and uplifting in a way that Disneyland could never be. As a prominent Dome advocate, Simon Jenkins, put it at the

18 Chris Smith, *op. cit.,* p. 127

time: "The dome is the envy of millennium organisers in Germany, France, Italy and America. . . . A nation with its feet on the ground must occasionally be swept up and given a glimpse of a far horizon."[19]

But the horizon was shrouded in mist. The proposed contents of the Dome remained worryingly vague. Increasingly onlookers were asked to admire it just as a *bold managerial concept*, like "New Britain" itself. And towards the end of 1999 the claims became both more grandiose and more commonplace, until it was said that the greatest of the Dome's managerial marvels was the fact that the chief executive, Jennie Page—in spite of having had less than four years to achieve success and having had to work on a salary of just £150,000 a year—would actually open it on New Year's Eve, *on time!*

And so she did. But the opening ceremony, portentously enough, was a palpable flop, the kind of old-fashioned cock-up which in a less credulous age would have been simply put down to rank bad management. The invited grandees were not sent entry passes beforehand and so were left queueing for them in the icy December rain at hastily-erected security checks. And the Dome, once open, proved a baffling disappointment; the combination of rows of electronic games and a trapeze display overhead reminding visitors less of an international testament to our nation's standing, than a tacky Las Vegas hotel lobby.

Indeed there was a growing suspicion that the opening had not been staged for the benefit of the indigenous population at all. It was a suspicion first voiced by the Arts Editor of *The Times*, who had stood on Blackfriars Bridge on New Year's Eve hoping to take part in the celebrations:

> It was when the fireworks ended that disillusion set in. Everyone was prepared for some queueing. But nobody realised just how many tube stations would be shut, or how catastrophic the knock-on effect would be. To force thousands of drenched families with small

children to wander helplessly around London in the
early hours of a winter morning was a monumental
failure of official planning. When we did finally board a
tube, having trudged two miles to Euston, the atmo-
sphere in our carriage was one of dejection rather than
elation. Only then did it dawn on me: the real reason
why we had all been lured to London by false promises.
We were there because the government needed a
gigantic crowd of unpaid extras for the World's TV
cameras. We were there to complete the illusion that
the British people had been inspired by their wonderful
leaders to mount "the world's best millennium party".
Having fulfilled this function we were then left to crawl
back to our holes as best we could . . . it seemed a
shoddy way to enter the 21st century.[20]

Dr William Acheson observed of the management of the
Dome's opening in the correspondence columns of *The
Times* (4 January 2000), "The event was unworthy of Great
Britain. All those concerned with its planning and
administration should be sacked."

Eventually, a few of them were, but not before there
had been a further memorable demonstration of the way
modern managerialism operates. For it was explained by
the Dome's managers that the visitors to the opening had
enjoyed a far better time *than they themselves had realised.* The
chief executive's explanation, in a letter circulated to the
broadsheet newspapers (6 January 2000), informed them
that, although it may not have been apparent to them while
they were having it, their experience had in "fact" been
"magical and unforgettable":

> In fact more than two thirds of our 10,500 guests
> arrived at the Dome at the times we had planned and all
> of them arrived before the royal party and the Dome
> opening celebration.
>   The vast majority of our guests entered into the
> spirit of the struggle of Stratford and we thank them

for their patience and understanding. Once they arrived at the Dome they experienced a magical and unforgettable night that has, together with the London celebrations, been acclaimed throughout the world as an overwhelming success.

The Dome's managers were soon confronted by a less tractable "fact". In less than a month it appeared that their enterprise faced bankruptcy, and they had urgently to request a further grant of £60,000,000 to ease their immediate "cash flow problems". The chairman of the New Millennium Experience Company, Sir Bob Ayling, sacked chief executive Jennie Page—who was thus able to devote more of her time to her work on the boards of Railtrack and Equitable Life—and in her stead appointed Pierre-Yves Gerbeau, 34, a Vice President of Disneyland Paris (no less) and a recent MBA graduate from the Sorbonne. The new chief executive immediately announced to the press that the Dome was "the best show in town", created a "more realistic" business plan which involved more staff, longer opening hours and dramatically-reduced projections of attendance—and within a few weeks was himself forced to ask for another £75,000,000. By May the New Millennium Experience Company was asking for yet another handout, this time of some £29,000,000. Bob Ayling now resigned the chairmanship.[21] and the expected admissions figure was lowered to between 6,000,000 and 7,000,000—*half* of the original government forecast,[22] and roughly the number of people who had visited the Great Exhibition of 1851 during its six month run.[23] Thus the Dome, created by modern

21 Later in the year Mr Ayling was removed from his position as chairman of British Airways, given a payment of just under £2,000,000 for "breach of contract" and awarded a pension of £260,000 a year.

22 In the event, the Dome attracted a total of 6,516,874 visitors, of whom 2,319,556 paid a reduced rate and at least 1,020,871 did not pay at all. Thus the full-payment admissions, 3,176,447, were in the event a *quarter* of what had been confidently forecast.

23 Virtually everyone entering the Great Exhibition paid the advertised rates. During its six-month run it did not open on Sundays, so the daily paying admission at 43,000 was roughly *five times* greater than the daily admission of full-paying entrants to the Dome.

management and flagship of "New Britain"—with its armies
of consultants, its 2,000-strong staff, its 300 managers and
its limp trickle of visitors, each one subsidised to the tune
of some £129—was for the rest of the millennial year reduced
to being just another tourist attraction sitting alongside such
cultural artefacts as the London Dungeon, Catherine
Cookson Country and the Robin Hood Experience.

In old-fashioned terms then the Dome was a clear
management failure. It had failed to meet any of its targets:
failed to attract customers, lost a huge amount of money
for its investors and greatly diminished confidence in its
product. Yet, in the shifting realms of modern management, it was no less "successful" than had been other
cultural activities controlled by the new managerialism. For
just as the Dome's managers had adjusted their market
strategies in the weeks following its opening—shifting
effortlessly from an insistence on the Dome's high educational purposes to an acknowledgement that its real
competitors were Disneyland and Alton Towers—and just
as they had repeatedly lowered their ticket sales targets, so
they now restrospectively redrafted the Dome's *aims and
purposes*. All along, it now appeared, the government had
been intent upon "regenerating" the Greenwich Peninsula!
While they had been distracting us with talk of the rebranding
of Britain, the state managers had been cunningly plotting
to redraw the economic map of London.[24]

But the failure of the Dome did not mean the end of
the rebranding processes. The commodification of the
national culture, for example, raged on unchecked.
"Resource", the state management unit which had
replaced both the former "Museums and Galleries Commission" and the short-lived "Museums, Libraries and
Archives Council" as one of the longer tentacles of the
culture ministry, ordered the museums and galleries under

24 Presumably the demolition of Wembley Stadium is part of the same secret plan.
But why has the government got it in for North London?

its control to make inventories of their cultural possessions which were "surplus to immediate requirements" and which could be sold off.[25] Resource's new chairman, Lord Evans, fresh from a commercial career and untainted by professional experience of museums or galleries, announced in May 2001 that he was "convinced that it has got to happen". (Comparisons with the sacking of the ancient library at Alexandria, with the destruction of the monasteries or with the more recent Nazi looting of the treasures of Prague were all beside the point, because, said Lord Evans, we were now in a quite new situation: we faced "the inexorable march of technology" and lived in a time of seismic social *change*. Ah, so!)

And the tainting of critical and aesthetic language with managerial jargon and mercantile values continued apace. The insistence that culture is an *industry*, and nothing more, meant that almost any kind of commercial activity could now stand alongside the traditional arts and humanities as a cultural equal—if not as a superior. Indeed, when we listened to the Senior Vice President of McDonald's UK describing the McDonald's "culture", we might well have been listening to a modern management consultant advising on the marketing of the Dome or of "New Britain": "Formal training about the business and operational procedures is underpinned by the cultural rub-off which keeps people very focussed on the brand."[26] Britain was now, in the eyes of its government, a brand just like McDonald's—although it must be admitted that the McDonald's spiel suggested a respect for history and tradition generally lacking in our state managers:

> We also never lose sight of our roots and once a year we hold what we call "Founder's Day", usually in October on a Friday, when all office employees,

25 This instruction even extended to the staff at the Tate Modern.
26 John Hawkes, "McDonald's UK: Balancing the Global Local Demands of the Brand", in Fiona Gilmore (ed.), *Brand Warriors*, p. 99

including those in the corporate and regional offices, and many of the partners in our supplier companies, leave their desks, put on a crew uniform and work in a restaurant for the day. Remembering what business we are in is an important part of our culture.

For "New Britain", in contrast to McDonald's, does not now have any historical roots—only cultural commodities which may be translated into hard cash.

And in the "New Britain" cultural commodities, being equal, are only differentiated by their varied price tags. Otherwise—in the absence of critical argument or the moderating sense of cultural history—all New British "cultures" are equal. That is what the government's "policy" of multi-culturalism presumably implies. And it is at this point that we can begin to see the great harm which modern managerialism is inflicting upon Britishness and the British culture. For in the "New Britain", within the new "multi-culturalism", where everything is judged by its immediate marketability rather than its value, and where no other criterion is allowed, there is no longer a basis for moral judgement, and no longer any means of effectively arguing with the state managers.

So when Mike Shaw proposed in 2001 to hold a St George's Day March through the streets of Leicester, he was able to tell his radio interlocutor[27] that he was acting entirely within the law and in accordance with the government's cultural policy, because his intention was to celebrate his national "culture", which was "English". The fact that Mr Shaw was the secretary of the National Front's East Midlands Branch, that Leicester is the only city in Britain in which the majority of inhabitants are black, and that the Leicester Police were suspicious of Mr Shaw's other motives becomes irrelevant. In "New Britain" the only questions which could legitimately be asked of him were questions such as "How many people will the event

27 *Today* Programme, BBC Radio 4, 14 April 2001

attract? Will your march increase local tourism, and will it show a profit?" In the managerialist state, quantifiable outcomes are the only criteria by which "success" is judged.

So it is worth saying the obvious, and asserting that even if the Greenwich Dome *had* been, in the older sense of the term, a managerial success, even if it had achieved its intended visitor figures of twelve and a half million people, and even if those people had all said they had enjoyed a good day out, *it would still have been a cultural disaster*. For modern managerialism, for all its pretension, is only a thin sliver of modern British culture, and what it considered to be the "Millennium Experience" of the British people was so shallow, so amoral and so mechanical, that it could not possibly have had any real vaue. For in the fully-managed state successes are no more *culturally* significant than failures. The much-hyped Tate Modern, for example, is an industrial success because the new gallery has exceeded its projected admission figures. But its *cultural* significance is another matter altogether. As Clive Bate has pointed out, managerial success must not be confused with artistic value:

> I do not begrudge the managers of Tate Modern their commercial success as they celebrate their first anniversary. But they should be very wary of counting it an equivalent artistic success.
>
> I found the exhibition skilfully laid out to chronicle the calamitous decline in artistic standards which took place during the 20th century. In 1900 painting and sculpture were noble fields of human endeavour which required the deployment of technique, imagination and taste. By 2000 this was quite clearly no longer the case.
>
> The responsibility for this change must be shared between the people who declare their products to be works of art, because they think they can fool some of the people all the time, and those who take their word for it without applying any evident objective standards. . . .
>
> To take pride in what has happened . . . as though it

were some kind of national achievement seems to me somewhat misguided, to put it mildly.[28]

Modern managerialism is itself a transient cultural manifestation, of a dull mechanical kind, which can talk in airy abstractions of quantifiable *things*, but never about people and the quality of their lives.

As the managerialists seek to wipe out the past and to obliterate all the meaningful cultural differences between us, the individual experience of our senses is continuously discounted. We are now *told*, in the crass language of modern managerialism, all that is happening to us and how we are responding to it. We now "access" the national culture "online", in a state-approved politically correct format. Our everyday experiences at work, at the shops or travelling have no significance until official reports tell us whether or not our employment is deemed sufficiently productive, whether "High Street demand" is rising or whether our transport systems are "meeting their targets".[29] New Britain, in addition to its daily grappling with "change", quite frequently "goes to war". These happenings are quite unlike previous wars. Rather than being declared in the old-fashioned way, they are instead *marketed* by intensive media campaigns. Meanwhile the British people, while being assured that it is they who are calling for and waging these conflicts, are wholly dependent upon the media to tell them how the "wars" are going and when, if ever, they have triumphed.[30] The result is that the British people are forced to inhabit two Britains—the everyday world of their senses, the "old country with a long history", with its myriad *un*official pleasures, and its

28 Letter to *The Times*, 17 May 2001

29 A Report on Europe's transport systems, published on 24 November 2001, pronounced what the British people had known for years, that their internal transport systems were the dirtiest, most expensive and least efficient in Europe. This, however, now became a managerial "fact", and made headline news.

30 At the time of writing, New Britain was at "war" with "Want", "Drugs" and "Terrorism", but neither defeat nor victory had been announced in any of these conflicts.

official "rebranded" counterpart, New Britain, the construct of modern management. Because the managerialists have hi-jacked so much of the English language, and because so much reportage is now in the form of managerial reports, it becomes increasingly difficult to find a truthful account of the way people now live—except, praise be, in the English novel! It is there, rather than in any of the turgid manifestations of government management-speak, that we can still find a sharp and reliable account of the *real world*.

9

The Real World:
Management in Literature

Managers themselves approach the rich world of literature with a strange ambivalence. On the one hand they are eager to use novels and plays as raw material for their own purposes. So Richard Olivier, son of the famous actor, can present courses for managers on Shakespeare's *Henry V* as a study in leadership ("participants told me they'd learned more from Henry than from any management guru"[1]). According to one recent volume, Shakespeare is full of lessons for the ambitious manager. Petruchio, who might seem a sexist bully, is actually "a model for today's corporate executive" faced with change, and Claudius's plotting against Hamlet is "another of Shakespeare's magnificent depictions of a successful business meeting".[2] Fiction can equally be seen as full of "models" and one volume opens with the reasonable claim that "The purpose of this book is to show how good novels can educate better managers." However, the actual approach demonstrates that "educate" is being used in the management sense: providing case studies to make predetermined points. It is assumed that novels and plays are there to

1 Olivier, who also offers courses on *Julius Caesar* and *Hamlet*, reported by Jim Pollard in *The Observer*, 21 January 2001

2 Norman Augustine and Kenneth Adelman, *Shakespeare in Charge: The Bard's Guide to Leading and Succeeding on the Business Stage*, 1999. Other recently published books include titles like *Shakespeare on Management*, by Paul Corrigan, and *Shakepeare's Lessons in Leadership and Management* by John Whitney and Tina Packer.

173

teach simple transferable lessons that the reader can "use", that they are full of "facts" and "knowledge" that "can be direct models for our undertakings" and help us "learn about . . . being a manager".[3] In this way the authors distort the nature of literature and the experience of reading it. As we suggested in chapter 3, most management writers seem to believe that language is unproblematic, neutral, transparent—that it simply reflects what they choose to call the "real world".

On the other hand, this desire to employ literature is balanced by a resentful feeling that most books and films unfairly misrepresent managers and entrepreneurs. The free-market Institute for Economic Affairs, in its study of the way that business is shown in English Literature, fears that enterprise may be stifled by the damning picture that emerges, and John Morris complains that "It is difficult to find positive and appreciative images of business in 20th-century English literature."[4] Indeed, the Director of the Institute suggests that ways should be found to give money to authors who will represent business and management as "honourable, creative, moral and personally satisfying".[5] It is frequently alleged that authors are ignorant of the world of management, and automatically opposed to it for social or political reasons.

Such criticisms can hardly apply to D. H. Lawrence, who perceptively records the complexities of managing industrial change in the early twentieth century in different novels, but particularly in *Women in Love* (1920). In that book, Gerald Crich is shown as an idealist who seizes on industrial management as "a vision of power", transforming his energy into will, enslaving the men who work under him: "Man's will was the absolute, the only absolute." Chapter 17 describes the pride with which he

---

3 B. Czarniawska-Joerges and P. Guillet de Monthoux (eds), *Good Novels, Better Management*, 1994
4 Arthur Pollard (ed.) *The Representation of Business in English Literature*, 2000, p. 137
5 *Ibid.*, Foreword

sees the hideous coal waggons and the sordid towns with their streams of blackened miners that represent his empire, and Lawrence repeats phrases like "subjugate to his will", "subordinate to him", "his instruments", "He was God of the machine." Gerald reduces social and moral issues to simple questions of function: "Was a miner a good miner? Then he was complete. Was a manager a good manager. That was enough. Gerald himself, who was responsible for all this industry, was he a good director? If he were, he had fulfilled his life. The rest was byplay." Earlier in the novel, when Birkin asked him what he lived for, Gerald responded: "I suppose I live to work, to produce something, in so far as I am a purposive being."

Far from being ignorant of business, Lawrence gets to the heart of managerial motives, and is not unsympathetic to Gerald's situation. Unlike some of the grasping business-men mentioned in Victorian novels, "It was not for the sake of money that Gerald took over the mines." Equally dangerously, though, "what he wanted was the pure fulfilment of his own will in the struggle with the natural conditions. His will was now, to take the coal out of the earth, profitably." His overriding concern to establish his will is vividly established in the celebrated early scene where he brutally forces his frightened Arab mare to face the noisy train of coal trucks. When Ursula later challenges him with his behaviour on that occasion, asserting the horse's "right to her own being", Gerald retorts that "that mare is there for my use . . . because that is the natural order . . . I can't help being master of the horse." Similarly he sees it as part of the "natural order" that he should be the master of the mines, and that the men should do his will.

Gerald is no caricatured monster, but Lawrence explores how his quest for greater managerial efficiency pushes him inevitably to dehumanise the workers. Gerald gets rid of the old clerks like "so much lumber" to replace them with "efficient substitutes" who would do as he wished. Contemptuous of humanitarianism and charity of the kind previously practised by his father, "in a thousand ways he cut down the expenditure, in ways so fine as to be hardly noticeable to the men. . . . But it saved hundreds of pounds every week for the firm." Gerald invests in new consultants, engineers and bureaucrats to bring in new machinery and working practices from America, centralising control in the name of efficiency and removing any autonomy that the men experienced.

> The working of the pits was thoroughly changed, all the control was taken out of the hands of the miners. . . . Everything was run on the most accurate and delicate scientific method, educated and expert men were in control everywhere, the miners were reduced to mere mechanical instruments. They had to work hard, much harder than before, the work was terrible and heartbreaking in its mechanicalness. But they submitted to it all. The joy went out of their lives, the hope seemed to perish as they became more and more mechanized. And yet they accepted the new conditions . . . Gerald was their high priest, he represented the religion they really felt. . . . The men were satisfied to belong to the great and wonderful machine, even while it destroyed them.

In Gerald's terms the changes are an obvious success. Output goes up and expenses down. He can invest in skilled men, engineers and under-managers, because "a highly educated man cost very little more than a workman", and saved the firm much more than the cost of his salary. "The whole system was so perfect that Gerald was hardly necessary any more." Lawrence did not live long enough to see how managerialism's "substitution of the mechanical principle for the organic" would spread from the industrial, manufacturing world into all spheres of life. However his perception stands as an ironic vision of, say, Henry Ford's River Rouge plant seen at the time as an embodiment of industrial democracy, a technological utopia, in which the goal was the constant perfecting of the industrial process itself. Ford subscribed to the principles of "Scientific Management" as developed by Frederick Winslow Taylor, holding that the manager's function was to discover "scientifically" the most efficient use of workers, thereby increasing productivity. Eliminating waste and matching man and machine came ultimately to mean the sort of robotizing of humans that Chaplin parodied with his tramp on the assembly line in *Modern Times* (1935) becoming a lunatic automaton.[4]

In the same way that the line of attack in the late nineteenth century shifted from individuals to the system, so in the middle and late twentieth century many writers moved from attacking figures like the ruthless Americanised manager to focus attention on the whole organisational or state apparatus within which he operated. Frequently associated with fear of Nazism (or later of what was happening in the Soviet bloc) serious and satirical novels analysed the ways in which news, information and image could be shaped for ends that no single individual had planned. Increasingly the manager merges with the bureaucrat, caught up in a system that turns the individual into a cog within a machine that is too complex to be explored. In many cases authors used visions of the future to express their concerns of the present. One critic has said that "clearly something happened to the British literary imagination in the 1930s to turn so many novelists' heads towards the future,"[5] citing a long list of works, most of them now only available in large libraries. Three mid-century novels, written from distinct positions, deserve to be examined here.

Aldous Huxley's *Brave New World* (1932) was motivated by horror at the worship of "progress" driven by the

4 John Dos Passos was just one of a number of American authors to attack the dire social consequences of Ford's adoption of mass-production methods. In his novel *The Big Money* (1937) he writes: "At Ford's production was improving all the time" but "at night the workmen went home grey shaking husks." It was left to Joseph Heller, in *Catch-22* (1961), to describe total war as big business gone mad.

5 Andy Croft in Christopher Norris, (ed.), *Inside the Myth*, 1984, p. 187

scientific speculations of H. G. Wells, Ivan Pavlov and others. He set out to discredit the notion that scientific managers applying behaviourist theories can provide a better world. Even by their own standards, Mustapha Mond and his World Controllers have failed through mismanagement, though this has in no way disturbed their confidence. The World State is a magnified version of Ford's motor plant, with individuals born artificially on an assembly line and trained for one job only in a caste system with managing Alphas at the top and Epsilons at the bottom. Aversion therapy involving electric shocks and loud noises is used to condition small children from the lower orders against liking books or pictures. The state is geared to the consumption of mass-produced goods: "Ending is better than mending" (or, as we would have it, "planned obsolescence"). Nature has been displaced by technology; individual identity is only permitted within a rigidly controlled collectivist setting. Huxley had perceived the connection between centralised bureaucratic authority and control (actually misuse or perversion) of the language that people use. Words like "mother", "family", "home", "love" and "romance" have become either meaningless or obscene. The Controller tells the boys that they are fortunate because "No pains have been spared to make your lives emotionally easy—to preserve you, so far as that is possible, from having emotions at all." Familiar terms like "new" and "old" are given fresh loadings, so that Shakespeare is prohibited, "because it's old. . . . We haven't any use for old things here." As Our Ford had pronounced, "History is bunk!" Similar redefinitions underlie comments of the Controller like "we believe in happiness and stability . . . you've got to choose between happiness and what people used to call high art."[6]

6 A lengthy essay defending the concept of "paradise engineering" and describing Huxley's novel as "one of the most insidious works of literature ever written" has been published by David Pearce on his BLTC web-site. He asks, "If it's technically feasible, what's wrong with using biotechnology to get rid of mental pain altogether?"

Still more pessimistic is George Orwell's dystopian satire *Nineteen Eighty-Four* (1949). Winston Smith, conscious all the time that the Thought Police might be scrutinising him and that Big Brother is watching, works in the Ministry of Truth. His job is the constant revision of past newspapers, to ensure that official predictions are always correct. When the forecasts are grossly wrong, "Winston's job was to rectify the original figures by making them agree with the later ones." The original newspapers are then destroyed and the new ones substituted in the official files. At times he has to create wholly imaginary heroic figures, like Comrade Ogilvy, who "would exist just as authentically and upon the same evidence as Charlemagne or Julius Caesar." The party slogan is: "Who controls the past controls the future; who controls the present controls the past." Colleagues undertake tasks like producing "definitive" versions of poems that have become ideologically offensive, issuing rubbishy sentimental books for the proles and working on the Newspeak Dictionary that is systematically eliminating some words from use. Syme looks forward to the time when knowledge of Oldspeak will have totally disappeared.

> The whole literature of the past will have been destroyed. Chaucer, Shakespeare, Milton, Byron— they'll exist only in Newspeak versions, not merely changed into something different, but actually changed into something contradictory of what they used to be.

The purpose of Newspeak is to ensure that ideas hostile to the régime can only be entertained in a vague, inarticulate way, and eventually to make all other methods of thought impossible. So Minipax (the Ministry of Peace) is concerned with war and a Joycamp is a forced labour or concentration camp.[7]

7 A similar approach, from a different political position, is seen in *Swastika Nights* (1937) by "Murray Constantine" (now known to be Katharine Burdekin). The novel describes a world divided between the Nazi and Japanese empires, in which all books, records and even monuments from the past have been destroyed, words like

Although it holds back the development of the narrative, the ideological centre of the novel is Winston's lengthy reading of Goldstein's book, provided by O'Brien, with its three chapters titled, "War is Peace", "Ignorance is Strength" and " Freedom is Slavery" (Part 2, chapter 9). Goldstein writes that by "the fourth decade of the twentieth century" (when Orwell was writing) "all the main currents of political thought were authoritarian." The new controlling aristocracy in a hierarchical society would consist of those who manage it: bureaucrats, technicians, organisers, publicity experts and politicians. Continuing war is essential "to use up the products of the machine without raising the general standard of living." Everything turns on *control*: the ability of those who manage the system to direct not only people's behaviour but the way they think and feel, as O'Brien finally and horrifyingly demonstrates to Winston.[8]

A similar, though perhaps less bleak, view of control, the dominance of "scientific" management and the subordination of workers to the machine, is given in Kurt Vonnegut's satire, *Player Piano* (1952). Vonnegut (himself a one-time public relations man for General Electric) traces the changes in the life of Dr Paul Proteus, at the beginning of the narrative "the most important, brilliant person in Ilium, the manager of the Ilium Works", and at the end a frustrated nonconformist. The book is placed in an American future, after a third world war and a second industrial revolution, when all routine manufacturing tasks are carried out by new machines and computers. People have been conditioned "by public relations and advertising men hired by managers and engineers" to believe that society should be

"marriage" and "socialism" have been expunged, and the totalitarian régime has ensured that only certain ways of thinking remain possible.

8 From within Stalin's Russia, Solzhenitsyn in works like *The First Circle* (1968) would ascribe the desire to control (by manipulating language and exerting different degrees of oppression) to fear and mistrust. "Distrust of the people was the dominating factor" of Stalin's life, and Solzhenitsyn suggests that he trusted only one man: Adolf Hitler.

organised in a rigid hierarchy, with managers and engineers at the top. In the first chapter we read that "This élite business, this assurance of superiority, this sense of rightness about the hierarchy topped by managers and engineers—this was instilled in all college graduates and there were no bones about it." As one of the characters adds, "And it's built on more than brain power—it's built on special kinds of brain power. Not only must a person be bright, he must be bright in certain approved, useful directions: basically management or engineering." The work of being a manager became much more pleasant when all was mechanised and there were no workers to manage.

In the name of efficiency, more and more workers find themselves replaced by robots. So it is that one of Paul's senior men, Bud Calhoun who runs the depot, invents a gadget that does his work better than he does, and automatically loses his job together with seventy-two others whose "job classification has been eliminated". At the centre of the whole operation is the master-computer EPICAC XIV, constantly busy deciding

> how many of everything America and her customers could have and how much they would cost. And it was EPICAC XIV who would decide for the coming years how many engineers and managers and research men and civil servants, and of what skills, would be needed in order to deliver the goods; and what IQ and aptitude levels would separate the useful men from the useless ones . . . .

Vonnegut explores the downside of the process: what it means to be categorised as useless, the frustration of human beings who used to get their sense of dignity from the jobs they did. Dr Halyard of the State Department explains to the visiting Shah of Bratpuhr, with a patronising chuckle, that the men he sees working on the road are not—as the Shah thought—slaves:

Citizens, employed by the government. They have the same rights as other citizens—free speech, freedom of worship, the right to vote. Before the war they worked in the Ilium Works, controlling machines, but now machines control themselves much better. . . . Less waste, much better products, cheaper products with automatic control. . . . And any man who cannot support himself by doing a job better than a machine is employed by the government, either in the Army or in the Reconstruction and Reclamation Corps.

In a chilling prophecy of our current obsession with appraisal, grading and league tables, Vonnegut describes how every college graduate's future is determined by the so-called Achievement and Aptitude Profile. At graduation, a machine took a student's grades and other performances and integrated them into one graph—the profile—recording levels for theory, administration, creativity, personality, and so on. "In mysterious, unnamed units of measure, each graduate was credited with having a high, medium, or low personality."

The views of the future presented in *Brave New World*, *Nineteen Eighty-Four* and *Player Piano* could be over-neatly contrasted as visions of Sci-Fi, Soviet and Capitalist systems, and yet what is most striking is the ultimate similarity between the three dehumanised, managerial worlds. All describe states in which individual choice and dignity, feelings and imagination, are squeezed out in the name of efficiency and uniformity. All suggest a bureaucratic organisation that deliberately cuts itself off from the past by manipulating language and marginalises or destroys the arts. All are rigidly hierarchical, and use grading and conditioning to maintain control.

The lengths to which manipulation might go are pushed to their limits in the recent futuristic fantasy that the all-powerful media tycoon, Sir Jack Pitman, conjures into reality in Julian Barnes's *England, England* (1998). It is a comic novel, but one at which we laugh uneasily. Sir Jack discusses his Island Project, with the management consultant to the elect, Jerry Batson, the consummate "adman, lobbyist, crisis-manager, image-rectifier and corporate strategist". They agree that England is a country with great accumulated cultural history that is eminently marketable, but that tourists are put off by the inconvenience of travelling around the multitude of sites. Their eminently simple solution is to recreate all that is essentially English on the Isle of Wight. When asked how the inhabitants will react to his plans, Sir Jack replies crisply: "It is not full of inhabitants; what it is full of is grateful future employees." Plans are developed to provide tourists who are tired of stress and anxious to "get back to nature" or to "the good old days" with a condensed, time-saving, Heritage, Quality Leisure experience. As the French intellectual on Sir Jack's coordinating committee demonstrates, with references ranging from Pascal through Saussure to Lévi-Strauss, "Nowadays we prefer the replica to the original."

Worldwide research comes up with a list of fifty quintessentially English items that might be included, like Robin Hood, pubs, cricket, the White Cliffs of Dover, Shakespeare, thatched cottages, marmalade, bowler hats, red buses, and so on. The key sites are replicated, staffed with employees who are to play Shakespeare, Francis Drake, Nell Gwyn, Dr Johnson and more anonymous rustics, outlaws and Chelsea Pensioners. Fast-food outlets offer roast beef and Yorkshire pudding, Lancashire hot-pot, fish and chips, bacon and eggs, shepherd's pie, bread-and-butter pudding. The helicopter tour of the island is "a sort of fast-forward version of England: one minute it was Big Ben, the next Anne Hathaway's Cottage, then the White Cliffs of Dover, Wembley Stadium, Stonehenge, one's own Palace and Sherwood Forest." The "traditional" rituals and festivals are as real as the organisers and participants choose to make them. Performance blends into reality:

The lolling shepherd must later be discovered in The Old Bull and Bush, where he would gaily accompany the pipe-playing gamekeeper in a selection of authentic country airs, some collected by Cecil Sharp and Percy Grainger, others written half a century back by Donovan. The haymakers would leave off their tourney of skittles to make menu suggestions, the poacher would explain his dodges, whereupon Old Meg crouching in the inglenook would lay down her clay pipe and disburse the wisdom of the generations.

By the end of the book, at the recently-invented "traditional" fête, Martha Cochrane is already finding reality and illusion blurred. Was Gibbet Hill once actually the site of a gallows? Was the uniformed policeman actually a lawman? She sees children entertaining themselves in front of the distorting mirrors:

> Even when they disbelieved, they also believed. The tubby, peering dwarf in the distorting mirror was them and wasn't them: both were true. They saw all too easily that Queen Victoria was no more than Ray Stout with a red face and a scarf round his head, yet they believed in both Queen Victoria and Ray Stout at the same time.

Martha's experience is like Winston's more sinister awareness of double-think in Orwell's *Nineteen Eighty-Four*: "To know and not to know, to be conscious of complete truthfulness while telling carefully constructed lies, to hold simultaneously two opinions which cancelled out, knowing them to be contradictory and believing in both of them . . . . "

This is why our laughter at the satire is uneasy. We recognise how close this is to the "Heritage Industry" and the rebranding of Britain described in the previous chapter. We are all too aware of our own double-thinking, and of the power of the media to create something between illusion and reality: the cricket international played under lights in coloured pyjamas, figures from TV soap operas opening events in the person of their characters rather than as themselves, sanitized war "news" made to look like action movies, the orchestrated mourning for Princess Di or celebrating the Queen Mother's hundredth birthday. When in *Nineteen Eighty-Four* Winston rewrites passages from past numbers of *The Times* to bring them in line with current policy, he reflects that "it was not even forgery. It was merely the substitution of one piece of nonsense for another . . . statistics were just as much a fantasy in their original version as in their rectified version."

It is perhaps significant that the manager figure who seems to appear most in the curriculum of university business courses is Vic Wilcox in David Lodge's comic novel *Nice Work* (1988), representing as it does the mutual incomprehension with which the academic and the industrial worlds view each other. Wilcox, the manager of a struggling engineering firm in Rummidge, is neatly balanced in the novel by Robyn Penrose, a lecturer in English at the local university, whose speciality is the industrial novel. The parallels are insistent: both work in institutions under financial pressure, both are in the grip of management structures and fear for their jobs (and at the end of the book Vic does, in fact, get sacked), and both are ignorant about the other's world. Brought together by the Industry Year Shadow Scheme, they are governed by their preconceptions—Vic's of soft academics ignorant of the "useful" world of work, and Robyn's of mindless, brutalising industry—and each is baffled by the other's viewpoint. When she intervenes in a meeting, he says that this is "a management matter in which you have no competence" and Robyn responds that "It's not a management matter, it's a moral issue." Predictably, though, as the novel goes on each learns something of the other's world and regards the other more warmly. "It was, perhaps, inevitable that Victor Wilcox and Robyn Penrose would end up in bed together in Frankfurt, though neither of them set out from Rummidge with that intention."

When it is Vic's turn to enter the university world, he is quickly able to dispel illusions that the collegiate world is any longer distinct from his own. As the book has demonstrated, the university is firmly within the grip of a rigid, hierarchical control system. Vic intervenes in a meeting with his view of what is happening: "Rationalisation is what you're talking about. . . . Cutting costs, improving efficiency. Maintaining throughput with a smaller workforce. It's the same in industry."[9] Same worlds or different worlds? The rather artificial happy ending (Victorian style, perhaps) sees Vic's family problems being resolved, his new venture being subsidized by a large loan from Robyn, who has come into money and had her job renewed. No future manager will be disturbed or challenged by reading this book, because it lacks satiric edge, and because Lodge manages to have it both ways. Vic may be mocked for his awful taste and for his conventional opinions, but comes out as a decent human being. The issue of work in his factory (or in the university) at a time of change is introduced but not explored. Lodge is uncommitted to any viewpoint; he shows how his story and characters can be deconstructed in academic criticism; and finally seems to mock the process of deconstruction itself.

How have writers of recent years responded to the challenge of representing managers and the business world, with such a lengthy tradition behind them? On one hand some have turned to ever wilder and more uncomfortable satire in the face of outrageous reality, like Terry Southern's extravagant images of crowds fighting in hot shit to grab dollar bills. On the other hand, some have taken to an ironic naturalistic mode of reporting, assuming that the absurdity of management's so-called real world is more ludicrous than any invented one might be.

9 The similarity of conditions in industry and the universities underlies Malcolm Bradbury's entertaining novella *Cuts*, 1987. The managers of the small provincial university in that book are cutting staff "with almost an excess of enthusiasm, as if they were longing for the day when the troublesome professoriate, the finicky

The absurdity of much managerial language and practice is so manifest that it cannot be caricatured, it is beyond satire. Increasingly novelists seem to become almost helpless recorders. So, when Justin Cartwright describes a business meeting, and the way that the spoken words flow meaninglessly over Anthony, his protagonist, they might be taken (and perhaps were) straight from recorded transcripts of some actual occasion. The confident Edward Jenkins reports on "ways of empowering our staff, to give them ownership of their own projects and allow implementation of management skills". His endless stream of modish jargon—"learning loop . . . proactive not reactive . . . ring-fence . . . feedback loop . . . activity versus process"—is unintelligible to Anthony: "The words, the torrents of words, are burying him. . . . They are words without substance, like crispbread." However, as soon as the managing director thanks Edward for his presentation, Anthony speaks up: "Brilliant. Very interesting shift of perceptual emphasis."[10]

Similarly, Jonathan Coe describes another all-too-common experience when professionals are obliged by their managers to give up important work in order to undergo some quite irrelevant management training. In his novel the participants in a luxurious hotel are senior psychiatrists, "whose attendance seemed to be a contractual obligation rigorously insisted upon by the managers and non-executive directors of their new hospital trusts." When the two course trainers appear, "Their faces were fresh and unformed, and they wore identical, closely-fitting Jaeger suits. Each appeared to be in his early twenties and had the vacantly shining eyes of the evangelical zealot." Tim had been in Minnesota, "where he had majored in Organizational Change at Duluth University"; Mark "boasted a diploma in Group Relations, Meeting Planning and Human Resource Development from the University of Milton Keynes."

lecturers, the annoying readers, would pass on to pastures new, mostly in the United States."

10 Justin Cartwright, *In Every Face I Meet*, 1995, pp. 40–3

"As qualified facilitators," said Mark McGuire, "our task during these sessions will be to engage you in a series of role-playing modules and creativity enhancement procedures."

"These methods have been tested and approved by some of America's most successful corporations," said Tim Simpson.

"The exercises you will be performing should not be regarded as a training programme *per se*," said Mark Mc-Guire. "Our aim is simply to open up your minds . . ."

"Stimulate creative thinking . . ."

"Engage your attention . . ."

"Embed key points and concepts for long-term retention . . ."

"And above all . . ." One more turn of the flip-chart, and then, in unison:

"MOTIVATE YOU FOR CHANGE."

"Now," said Tim Simpson, "does anyone have any questions?"

Most of the audience seemed too dazed and bewildered to ask questions at this stage, so the facilitators divided them up into groups of five and explained that the first exercise would provide a relaxed forum in which introductions could be made.

The psychiatrists have to do this, wearing "the silly hats" that the two facilitators have brought; then they have to "find ways of arranging six matchsticks so as to make different combinations of equilateral triangles"; and "unblock their latent creativity channels"; they must "make personalized sculptures out of pipe-cleaners"; and then play a game called "Modify that Paradigm", which involves cutting up coloured advertisements and re-assembling the pieces "into an original collage". When some of the elderly and highly qualified participants begin to complain, Dr Dudden protests that "The success of American business is built on events like this."

"Oh, what bullshit," said Dr Myers. "For one thing, providing health care is not a business. And secondly, American business success is a myth. Look at their national debt. You don't find the Germans or the Japanese messing around with matchsticks and pipe-cleaners during their working hours. On the contrary, this sort of thing shows you exactly what's wrong with the Americans: their pathetic infantilism."[11]

Comment on passages like these becomes superfluous. The suspicions of businessmen recorded at the beginning of this chapter are largely justified. Authors *are* antagonistic to their world, but not because of ignorance, snobbery or political bias. If novels and plays are to succeed, then they must offer valid understanding of human relations within a particular social system. That is what the authors cited here have done. Our point is that, directly or by implication, they offer their criticisms of managers and management systems far more cogently than any sociological analysis or factual commentary could do.

11 Jonathan Coe, *The House of Sleep*, 1997, pp. 251–62

Bursting the Managerial Bubble

It is a wrench to leave the clear outlines of the English novel and turn back to the blurred images of modern managerialism. Although no reasonable person had imagined that management could ever become an art, even the hopes that it might at least become some kind of applied science have been dashed. For management has not, in any sense, evolved into a scientific system. Indeed, as we have tried to show, modern management is more a matter of attitude and spin than a systematic application of principles which are rationally derived. The modern manager may still speak of a "mission" to manage "change", to "drive things forward" and "reach objectives", but for all that purposeful, tough-sounding jargon the practice does not seem to connect with the real world. And over recent years it has become ever more clear that the *principles* of modern management—compounded as they are of political pieties and dubious economic laws— are of significance only because so many people persist in thinking that they are.

Everyone will agree that the political targets towards which modern managers "drive" their strategies change with the wind. Nothing is so forlorn as yesterday's political correctness.[1] However, the fact that economic laws are *also*

1 In the not very distant past, "worker representation" in management was the height of political correctness. Now, amongst other things, it is "equal opportunities". Soon we may follow the USA in legislating for "positive discrimination" in management. It will be interesting to see which race or party we choose to discriminate in favour of.

shaped by history and culture, and change from age to age and between one country and another, may not be so obvious. Yet the laws, and the nature, of economics change from decade to decade. It is useful to recall that until quite recently the study of economics was not primarily concerned with formulating "laws" at all. In the universities, as Dr Kadish has pointed out, economic analysis was regarded as a useful adjunct to historical enquiry—something to check or modify a merely narrational account of the past:

> Economic theory, as well as political philosophy were regarded as a response to, and an attempt to explain, specific historical conditions rather than exercises in abstract speculation on ideal conditions. Consequently the teaching of economics was often a simple extension of the responsibilities of the history tutor or college lecturer.[2]

Modern economics is altogether more ambitious. It puts forward its abstract speculations as formulae both to "explain" events and to predict behaviour in the real world. Yet a study of those areas in which economists authoritatively pronounce—the wisdom of raising or lowering interest rates, say, or the kind of investment needed genuinely to regenerate an inner city economy—will suggest that the real world rarely if ever disports itself according to standard economic formulae. And modern economic terms do not transcend cultural boundaries in the way scientific terms, and laws, inevitably do. Temperature is measured in the same way in India as in Britain but, as J. K. Galbraith has clearly shown, the difference in their cultures means that the "laws" of "economic efficiency" are quite different in each country.[3] Again, the Second Law of Thermo-

2 Alon Kadish, *Historians, Economists and Economic History*, 1989, p. 5

3 Professor Galbraith has pointed out that it is economically efficient in India to employ twelve men to cut a lawn with scissors. In Britain it is economically efficient to employ one person with a motor mower. For an elaboration of this see J. K. Galbraith, *The World Economy Since the Wars*, 1994, pp 172–83.

dynamics is as demonstrably true in Hong Kong as it is in the USA, but the notion of "economic value" in Hong Kong rests upon quite different criteria from those holding sway in Wall Street.[4] Further examples are easy to find. Culture and history shape our economic "laws", not the other way around.

So modern managerialism, largely dependent upon fashionable political and economic saws, has no rational basis. Its axioms, though sometimes masquerading as scientific laws, neither adequately describe nor effectively shape events in the real world. They are expressed in smeary abstractions which take no account of the richness and complexity of the human world, and which cannot usefully be applied to it. A few of modern managerialism's failures in cultural realms—the "rebranding" of Britain, the "Millennium Experience", the creation of the National Centre for Popular Music, trying to turn the arts into "creative industries"—have already been discussed in these pages. But such failures have in recent years been matched by equally damning failures in ordinary commercial realms, in businesses where common-sense management was badly needed, but where the adoption of modern managerialist practices has proved disastrous. Recent examples range from the cyclonic rise and fall of the dot.com industries to the accumulated troubles of the national railway system.

In October 2000, in good weather, a mid-day train going north from King's Cross was derailed at Hatfield, killing four of the passengers and injuring thirty more. On-the-spot investigation revealed that the cause of the accident was not Irish terrorism (as was at first suggested by the spin doctors) but the failure of the privatised rail company, Railtrack, to have properly maintained the track. Further

4 The Dow Jones Industrial Average, the New York Stock Exchange's arbiter of economic value, jumps between 10 and 374 points every time an American golfer called Tiger Woods plays in a tournament. When he doesn't appear the share index falls by the same amount (*The Times*, 15 May 2001). On the Hong Kong Stock Exchange prices are not affected by Mr Woods.

investigation showed at least two hundred other stretches of line on which it was no longer safe for trains to run at their accustomed speed. Belatedly, and with hefty government assistance, Railtrack set about repairing the faults, and the British railway system descended into chaos. For six months and more the trains, filled with long-suffering commuters and uncomprehending tourists, slowed by working parties on the line, by energy failures and a host of new speed restrictions, crawled to hastily-revised timetables which were less an advertisement for "New Britain" than reminiscent of the way patched-up steam trains had run during the blackouts and coal shortages of the 1939–45 War.

Railtrack thus offered a useful illustration of the way modern management systems corrode and destroy the enterprises they ostensibly support. It appeared that necessary maintenance and repair had been neglected in the quest for short-term managerial "outcomes". The situation had been allowed to run out of control because the railways were operated by managers who knew everything about managerial abstractions—the minutiae of attracting share capital, assembling a well-qualified managerial team, paying good dividends and promoting a good public image—but nothing about the mundane practicalities of what was needed to maintain railway tracks in safe working order.[5] Yet to modern managerialists such priorities did not seem untoward. At the height of the crisis, the Deputy Prime Minister, John Prescott, sent his own representative into Railtrack, not to question its being, nor to examine its technical competence, but to ask whether its *management* was of the right standard. Railtrack's erstwhile chief executive, Gerald Corbett, had meanwhile walked away with a golden handshake of more than £1 million. In a radio interview,[6] he brightly announced

5 In May 2001 it was announced that Railtrack was to return to the old British Rail system of employing local engineers with experience to check and mend its tracks.

6 *Today* programme, BBC Radio 4, 17 November 2000

that he was looking forward to playing more golf, losing some weight and travelling to India, before "going forward" to his next managerial challenge . . .

There was some mild apprehension over Mr Corbett's remarks, not least from other services which, viewing the shambles on the railways, feared that they might turn out to be the next challenge in his managerial sights. Other railway travellers expressed themselves more trenchantly:

> It seems odd that the man in charge of Railtrack is traditionally an ignoramus when it comes to trains. Mr Gerald Corbett, who recently resigned, was head of a hotel group when he was appointed. His predecessor, Sir Robert Horton, was a retired BP executive, while the new man, Mr Steven Marshall, is something to do with the drinks industry. This seems to be the way most management operates these days.[7]

It seemed that even a spectacular failure such as this could not dent the widespread belief that a modern manager does not need to know anything much about what is being managed. The Hatfield disaster only served to reinforce the general understanding that everything can be improved by having more modern management, not less, coupled with the underlying belief that "management" is the same quantifiable entity, whether it is a private industry or a public service which is being managed.

At the time of the 2001 election, two things were apparent about the public services. The first was that over previous decades they had largely been removed from democratic control, and had instead been made the responsibility of managerial bureaucracies. The Health Authorities, for example, had been restructured, with a reduction in the number of elected representatives sitting on them, and a corresponding increase in commercial and business managers. Urban Development Corporations, comprised for the most part of unelected business executives, had

7 Richard Ingrams, writing in *The Observer*, 26 November 2000

been given budgets from public funds of more than £200 million and been handed responsibility for a swathe of public services. Every region also had its Training and Enterprise Councils, consisting largely of businessmen and women, and also dispensing substantial public funds. So by 2001, in the words of an experienced British politician, local government had "been reduced to little more than a tier of administration".[8] On the other hand increased centralisation had not meant greater powers for the elected parliament. According to another observer, "The House of Commons begins to look like a chamber on the verge of being pensioned off to enjoy a quiet life."[9] Power over the erstwhile public sector services increasingly rested with that shadowy coagulate of like-minded bureaucrats whom we have termed *modern managers*.

The second thing which was clearly apparent was that in health, education, social services and the arts modern management *was not working*. Schools and departments of social services, stifled by the ever-mounting bureaucracy, found it increasingly difficult to recruit staff, even when the state offered handsome bribes to new recruits.[10] Doctors, equally exasperated by bogus industrial "targets" and mounds of unnecessary paperwork, threatened to leave the National Health Service *en masse*. The churches, in spite of rewriting the scriptures in "marketable" terms, and producing strategies for the better management of the Christian faith,[11] continued to lose worshippers and influence. The effects of state managerialism were so obviously destructive of the British cultural fabric that even the normally compliant world of the subsidised arts became cynical:

8 Tony Benn, "How Democratic is Britain?" in Keith Sutherland, (ed.), *The Rape of the Constitution?*, Thorverton, 2000, p. 51

9 Nevil Johnson, "Parliament pensioned off?" in *ibid.*, p. 162

10 On the principle that only money talks, teachers were to be welcomed into their first jobs with a cash payment called a "Golden Hello".

11 A 2001 report, commissioned by the Archbishops of Canterbury and York, said that the Church of England would be best-served if its senior members were trained in management. It was called, without intended irony, *Resourcing Bishops*.

What *is* incontestable is that the language of arts policy and management—discourse, shall we call it—has been hideously bureaucratised under new Labour. The new management-speak thesaurus must be ever at hand if Government or its funding quangos are to "dialogue" seriously with you. If you want "face time" with a minister or senior civil servant, then you should brush up your cant. "Quality face time"—in which the minister actually listens to what you say—requires cant of the more advanced kind.[12]

Yet it took more than ridicule, or repeated failure, to divert the managerialists from their course. As he entered the last week of his thoroughly-managed election campaign, Mr Blair was asked what he intended to do about the gathering crises in the public services. He replied that in his second administration he would "drive forward" reform by bringing a "top businessman" into the heart of Whitehall:

I want to focus the centre of government on delivery. I will establish what will in effect be a policy delivery unit which will be in the Cabinet Office but the head of it will report directly to me. We will use that to make sure across the public services that we're driving through the change and reform that is necessary.[13]

"Change", "reform" and "delivery"—but of what? When described in these managerial terms even the flesh and blood of the New Labour cabinet seemed like a theoretical abstraction. How does one "focus" a government's "centre"? After a campaign in which politicians of all major parties had striven to sound capable and concerned without actually saying anything meaningful, Mr Blair was unenthusiastically returned to Downing Street by the lowest percentage turnout of voters for more than eighty years. And all went on much as before.

12 John Tusa, "A is for Artspeak in New Labour Lingo", *The Times*, 12 May 2001

13 *The Times*, 1 June 2001. Mr Blair, on taking office in 1997, had cut down on state bureaucracy by dissolving the Government Efficiency Unit, which of course from 1992 to 1997 had been chaired by a prominent businessman.

So the question we must finally confront is this. If modern managerialism achieves so few of its intended targets, and yet indirectly does harm to so much of British life, why does it still hold sway, and why are its adherents still listened to with apparent respect? Why do Britain's churches, schools, social services, the arts—real parts of real life—still allow themselves to be drawn into its web? By what power does modern managerialism persuade so many people to be complicit in their own destruction? What kind of cultural manifestation *is* it?

Are its followers perhaps *possessed*? Is modern managerialism a kind of religious cult in which large numbers of British people willingly sacrifice their judgement and common sense, in return for a sense of belonging, of being party to some preordained *purpose*? History, as the wise Dr Mackay wrote a century and a half ago, contains many warnings that whole societies can willingly succumb to a single overwhelming delusion:

> In reading the history of nations, we find that, like individuals, they have their whims and their peculiarities; their seasons of excitement and recklessness, when they care not what they do. We find that whole communities suddenly fix their minds on one object, and go mad in its pursuit: that millions of people become simultaneously impressed with one delusion, and run after it, till their attention is caught by some new folly more captivating than the first. . . . At an early age in the annals of Europe its population lost their wits about the sepulchre of Jesus, and crowded in frenzied multitudes to the Holy Land; another age went mad for fear of the devil, and offered up hundreds of thousands of victims to the delusion of witchcraft. At another time, the many became crazed on the subject of the philosopher's stone, and committed follies till then unheard of in its pursuit.[14]

14 Charles Mackay, *Extraordinary Popular Delusions and the Madness of Crowds*, 1841; preface to the 1852 edition, pp. XIX, XX

We cannot consider our own time immune from such mass hysterias. One authority recently insisted that "psychological plagues at the end of the twentieth century are all too real".[15] Certainly, in the way they constantly refer to the need for "global capitalism"[16] and the forces of "change" to be confronted and *countered*, modern managerialists seem to be conforming to a recognisable psychological norm:

> Contemporary hysterical patients blame external sources—a virus, sexual molestation, chemical warfare, satanic conspiracy, alien infiltration—for psychic problems. A century after Freud, many people still reject psychological explanations for symptoms; they believe psychosomatic disorders are illegitimate and search for physical evidence that firmly places cause and cure outside the self.[17]

And if many people are indeed possessed by belief in a managerial cult, then it is easier to explain why its numerous failures do not seem to dent belief in its validity and power. As Dr Thomas remarks:

> It is a feature of many systems of thought, and not only primitive ones, that they possess a self-confirming character. Once their initial premises are accepted, no subsequent discovery will shake the believer's faith, for he can explain it away in terms of the existing system. Neither will his convictions be weakened by the failure of some accepted ritual to accomplish its desired end, for this too can be accounted for. Such systems of belief possess a resilience which makes them virtually immune to external argument.[18]

Which sounds like the kind of mind-set which, in order to "successfully" control the 2001 outbreak of Foot and Mouth disease and "successfully" to keep the countryside

15 Elaine Showalter, *Hystories: Hysterical Epedemics and Modern Culture*, New York, 1997, p. 4
16 See Noreena Hertz, *The Silent Takeover: Global Capitalism and the Death of Democracy*, 2001
17 Showalter, *op. cit.*, p. 4
18 Keith Thomas, *Religion and the Decline of Magic*, revised edition, 1997, p. 641

open for tourists, refused to allow farm animals to be vaccin-
ated against the disease, but instead embarked upon a
campaign of mass-slaughter with 12,000 healthy animals
being destroyed for every one infected, *and all without ending
the outbreak*? And how can it be that the British people
tolerated the kind of spin doctoring which suggested that
this was a well-managed and effective action? Surely, we
must all be possessed.

It is tempting to consider the possibility, but even the
writing and publication of this book demonstrates that it is
not the case. For genuine cults are intolerant of *any* kind of
opposition. Whereas it was highly dangerous, if not impossible, to speak out against the persecution of witchcraft, it is quite easy for the present authors to write about
the foolishness of modern managerialism, and to engage
in public debate on the subject, without fearing arrest or
imprisonment.

Apart from anything else, there is growing safety in
numbers, for they are by no means alone in their opinions.
In the newspapers there is now open speculation about the
curious hold that modern managerialism still has upon
many of our leaders:

> The cult of management is profoundly mystifying. The
> discipline itself seems utterly fraudulent, based on
> illusion and incomprehension. The illusion is that the
> world can be made safe if you reduce everything to
> numbers. Incomprehension lies at the heart of the thing:
> if you don't understand, either intuitively or objectively,
> the culture or process you are trying to "manage", then
> you try and remove the bits you can't grasp and replace
> them with bits you can. It's like watching an improperly
> trained surgeon trying to cure a patient by removing the
> liver, spleen, kidneys and lungs, and replacing them with
> boils and cysts—the things he *does* know about—from a
> gunny sack on the floor at his feet.[19]

19 Michael Bywater, "Managing to take the Great out of Britain", *The Guardian*, 12
February 1999

Criticism of the regressive practices of modern management, and the harm they inflict, is nowadays as likely to appear in the business section as on the features page:

A mountain of research now demonstrates beyond ambiguity that there is a link between performance and good management of people.

Unfortunately, the government's enthusiasm for an evidence base for medicine doesn't stretch to its own management. Instead of mandating a progressive, decentralised, people-centred management approach for the knowledge age, its management methods for schools, universities and the NHS represent a decisive step backwards.

According to the *Economist*, the public sector now has 600 separate targets to juggle, a number probably unmatched since pre-*glasnost* Soviet Union. But targets don't work. Instruments of mass-production, they are centralised and disempowering, turning managers into numbers-chasers and teachers, doctors and professors into petty bureaucrats. They quickly become a form of tyranny.[20]

Is modern managerialism then a *political* system, a means of exercising political control? Is managerialism a political "tyranny" rather than a religious "cult"?

In the way it proceeds modern managerialism has more than a passing resemblance to the establishment of a political dogma. In its simultaneous "rebranding" of national economy and national culture, in its determination to regard wealth as the sole criterion of value, in the way it sets industrial "targets" for both the spiritual and material world and then insists upon state "strategies" to achieve them, its techniques clearly resemble those used in dictatorships everywhere, and in the former USSR in particular. Perhaps the closest comparison is with the glum orthodoxy which drove the Soviet bureaucrats, and which

20 *The Observer*, 3 June 2001

for several decades possessed the minds of many of the British chattering classes. It is perhaps Marxism that modern managerialism most nearly resembles. Like Marxism, it is capable of infiltrating and distorting the workings of many kinds of organisation. Like Marxism it works primarily by colonising and colouring everyday language. And like Marxism it asserts that all creation, imagination and cultivation stem from measurable material processes. When we look back at the words of a prominent British advocate of modern managerialism, their kinship with old-fashioned Marxist dogma is striking:

> The Creative Industries Taskforce has already started on a wide-ranging programme of work. We are mapping creativity in Britain, and assessing its economic trends and potential. . . . We are looking ahead to ensure that the UK industries are properly equipped to exploit fully the potential of new technologies.[21]

For Mr Smith is unashamedly and dogmatically *materialist*. In the future, Smith seemed to be saying, everything in Britain—all love, all art and all faith—will derive from our "creative industries" fully exploiting "the potential" of the "new technologies"—as mechanistic a view of cultural evolution as could be found anywhere in history, and in any kind of political régime.

That art, faith and love do *not* derive from a materialist base is obvious to everyone except the die-hard materialists of Marxism and of modern managerialism. It was obvious even to Marx himself:

> It is well known that certain periods of high development in the arts stand in no direct connection with the general development of society, nor with its material basis and the general structure of its organisation.[22]

21 Chris Smith, *Creative Britain*, 1998, p. 32
22 *Marx and Engels on Literature and Art*, ed. L. Baxandall and S. Morawski, St Louis, 1973, p. 134

But the belief that art and culture derive solely from material bases, managerial structures and the "general development of society" was still firmly bolted in to the New Labour government's mind, even after Mr Smith's departure from high office.

After the 2001 election a brand-new Culture Minister continued to run along the same well-worn grooves. The Culture Ministry was enlarged (by adding gambling and horse-racing to its cultural responsibilities) but Tessa Jowell, the new Minister, was still constrained by the old materialist dogma. She found herself bound by forty-four "cultural pledges" which had been publicly made by the previous administration. One of the more surprising among them was a promise to computerise the entirety of the national culture, so that it could be more easily "accessed". To achieve this, the government was pledged to spend £150 million on a new website, which was to be called "Culture Online". In a stroke therefore, the Ministry had made British culture accessible to all! It took Julian Spalding to observe that commodifying culture in this way, and linking it with a quantitative notion of "creativity", drained it of all significance and made it value-free. It detached modern "culture" from tradition, and ludicrously implied that art was "an eternal present of creativity, free of history".[23]

How can these fatuities be brought to an end? How can we prick the monstrous bubble of modern managerialism, and restore people to their senses? It will not be the work of a few moments. Neither cool logic nor passionate complaint are by themselves likely to bring the managerial edifice suddenly crashing down. As Dr Mackay remarks, "Men, it has been said, think in herds, while they only recover their senses slowly, and one by one."[24]

23 Julian Spalding, "No Room for History in the Labour Culture", *The Times*, 26 May 2001
24 Charles Mackay, *op. cit.*, p. xx

So success must come slowly. And its arrival will depend upon increasingly exercising our individual critical judgement (a term which, like "excellence", "quality" and "value", may not be appropriated and bestowed by the Ministry of Culture). It is only by exercising that judgement that people may, one by one, again come to their senses. Then they may recognise afresh that it is sensible for those who manage to have some experience and knowledge both of what they are managing and of the people whom they control. They may question the current obsession with "efficiency", rejecting it when it becomes an abstraction, used without regard for the human needs of workers and customers. Above all, they may reject the bland assumption that all human activities have their price tag, and that even "knowledgeable activity *must* be sold like other commodities to be of value."[25]

We must rekindle genuine debate in Britain. Every kind of twentieth-century dictatorship strove where it could to control the media and to stifle critical voices. Some of the darkest moments in those decades occurred when dissenting voices were suddenly silenced—when the German universities collapsed before the Nazis, or when the Czechoslovakian radio stations were silenced by Soviet tanks in 1968. It is surely even more terrible when those with responsibility for maintaining critical dialogue —the universities, the BBC, the arts councils and the schools—*needlessly* capitulate to the forces of cant and mercantilism. For though physically crushed, the German universities, and the Prague radio station, rose again. By contrast, as the leaders of Britain's arts, services and education system have in recent years so often been willing partners to their own managerial destruction, it is not easy to see from whence their resurrection may come. It will not be a simple matter to goad them back into critical life.

25 Craig Pritchard in C. Pritchard *et al.*, (eds), *Managing Knowledge*, 2000, p. 233

In order that we may once more engage in creative argument, it is essential that the English language be rescued from the robotic grasp of the bureaucrats, with their conceited assumption that they alone inhabit some "real" world. For the materialists have heaped such scorn upon so many honourable terms in the English language that it is now hard to use them without apology. In the managerial lexicon, British citizens may no longer be commended for being *gentle, amateur, scholarly, patriotic, modest, unambitious, dutiful, charitable* or *sportsmanlike*. To be taken seriously modern Britons must be *ambitious, entrepreneurial, hard-nosed, interventionist, focussed, driven, work-centred* and, above all, *committed* to modern managerialism. We must not allow ourselves to be deflected by the *image-makers, spin-doctors* and *rebranders* of multi-national corporations and of the managerialist state. It is time to restore a language which conveys a different set of values. To start with, we should make *modern managerialism* itself a term of high abuse. By constantly stigmatising wasteful bureaucracy, spin-doctoring and empty "strategising" with the hated phrase, by pointing repeatedly to the crass and wasteful consequences of using "modern management" techniques (and contrasting them with proper, old-fashioned management) we must together ensure that the words *modern managerialism*, whether used in Parliament, common room, tap room or Synod, soon call forth nothing but derision from all thinking people. We hope this book helps to bring that happy day closer.

Index

Acheson, William, 165
"active citizenship", 134–5
Advisory Committee on the Supply and Education of Teachers , 124n6
Allen, Roger E., 62
Alpha Movement, 54, 143
Alton Towers, 167
Alvesson, M. and Wilmott, H., 76n8
Amis, (Sir) Kingsley, 57n8
Annual Report 2000, 53
Arnold, Matthew, 107
Arnott, Margaret A., and Raab, Charles D., 119n4
Arts Council of England, 17, 40, 110
Arts Council of Great Britain, 22–3, 96, 100, 101–2, 103, 105
"arm's length principle", 22, 122
ASDA, 99
Association of Teachers in Management, 70
Augustine, Norman and Adelman, Kenneth, 173n2
Ayling, (Sir) Bob, 166

Bach, J. S., 92
Bailey, Lucy, 119n4
Ball, (Sir) Christopher, 43
Baker, (Lord) Kenneth, 125–6, 129, 136
Barnes, Julian, 182–5

Baxandall, L. and Morawski, S., 202n22
Barnardo, Dr, 13,14
Bate, Clive, 170
Bayley, Stephen, 163
BBC, 17, 22, 149–50
"beacon schools", 134
Benetton, 38
Benn, Tony, 196n8
Better Schools, 125n7
Birkett, Dea, 135n21
Birmingham, University of, 82
Birt, (Lord) John, 10n1, 17
Bishop Grosseteste University College, 148
Black Papers, 123
Blair, Tony, 24–6, 53n5, 106–7, 128, 130, 156, 197
Blanchard, Ken, 60
Blunkett, David, 67, 128–30, 136–7
Boot, Jesse, 13
Bottery, Mike, 128, 131
Boyle, David, 30n2
Bradbury, Malcolm, 186n9
Brendon, Piers, 37n10
Bridge, David, 149
British Council, 22
British Educational Management and Administration Society, 117
British Film Institute, 100
British Public Library Service, 38–9, 110

British Rail, 18, 23
British Telecom, 115
Britannic Assurance, 135
Brockbank, Peter, 34
Brooke, (Lord) Peter, 104
Brown, Gordon, 159
Burdekin, Katharine, 179n7
Burnham, James, 19n13
Butler, (Lord) R. A., 18
Byers, Stephen, 128
Byrt, William, 72n4
Bywater, Michael, 200

Callaghan, (Lord) James, 123
Cambridge, University of, 26–7,
    82–3
Cartwright, Justin, 187
Cathedral Measures (1999), 149
Catherine Cookson Country, 167
Caulkin, Simon, 130n16
CCTV systems, 30
"change", 24, 25–6, 34, 36, 168,
    171, 188, 193
Chater, Mark, 146–7
Cherry Blossom Boot Polish, 38
Church of England, 142, 143–4,
    146, 148–9, 151
City University, 67n19, 82
Clark, Timothy and Salaman,
    Graeme, 61n14
Coe, Jonathan, 187–189
Cole, (Sir) Henry, 163
Columbia University, 10
Collins, Phil, 110
Colman's Mustard, 33
Commission for Health Improve-
    ment, 51
Connaught Rooms, 109
Consignia, 39
Constable, John, 53
Cook, Thomas, 13, 36–8
Coopers and Lybrand, 113n10
Corbett, Gerald, 194–5
Cornwall, proposed University
    of, 27
Corrigan, Paul, 173n2
Cossens, (Sir) Neil, 11–2

Crafts Council, 100, 103
Creative Industries Taskforce, 111
Croft, Andy, 177n5
Cultural Business Support for
    South Yorkshire Unit, 112–3
Culture and Creativity: The Next Ten
    Years, 12
Culture Online, 203
Cunningham, Jack, 107
Cupitt, Don, 141, 142n2
Czarniawska-Joerges, B. and Guil-
    let de Monthoux, P., 174n3
Daniels, Ardha and Thomas,
    Alan B., 75n7
Davies, Nick, 175
Dearing, (Lord) Ron, 83
Dearing Report, 127
Decade of Evangelism, The, 143
Demos, 160
Department for Education and
    Employment, viii, 111, 134, 159
Department of Culture, Media
    and Sport, 40, 159
Department of National Herit-
    age,104–6
Dewey system, 99
Diana, Princess of Wales, 12, 109,
    185
Dickens, Charles, 52, 131
Disneyland Paris, 163, 167
Dos Passos, John, 177n4
dot.com industries, 92, 193
Drucker, Peter, 17
Dunham, Jack, 118n2

Earth Centre, Doncaster, 114n10
East Bassetlaw, 55–6
Eaves, Morris, 95n1
Economic Importance of the Arts in
    Britain, The (1988), 53–4
Education Act (1988), 125–6
Education for Management: Manage-
    ment Subjects in Technical and Com-
    mercial Colleges, 70–1, 73
Elgar, Edward, 53
Elizabeth II, Queen, 160–1
Emin, Tracey, 108

English Heritage, 11–12
English Regional Producing Theatres, 40–1
Equitable Life, 166
e–university, proposed, 41–2
European Economic Community, 19–20
European Union, 19
Evans, (Lord) Michael, 167–8

"fact", 29–31, 52–4, 165–6, 171, 174
Faith and Order Committee Report (1999), 148
Farnham, David and Horton, Sylvia, 21
FCUK, 38–9
Fender, Brian, 44n18 and n19
Ferguson, R., 119n4
Festival of Britain, 1951, 161–2
Film and Media Board, 110
Financial Services Authority, 135
Ford, Henry, 176–7
Ford Motor Company, 99
Fraser, (Lady) Antonia, 98
Freeman, J. S., 146n10
Freeman, R. Edward, 58n9
Freud, Matthew, 35–6
Furlong, Monica, 148n12
Future of the British Civil Service, The, 24–25

Galbraith, J. K., 192–3
GCHQ, 20
Gephart, Robert P., 59n12
General Electric, 180
Gerbeau, Pierre-Yves, 166
Golding, David and Currie, David, 76n8, 77n9
Goldsmiths College, 82
Government Efficiency Unit, 197n13
"great debate", the, 123
Great Exhibition 1851, 163, 166
Greenwich, 162–3, 167
Grey C. and Mitev, N., 76n8
Grey, Christopher, 77

Gulbenkian Foundation, 99

Habgood, John, 146, 148, 152
Hammer, Mike and Champy, James, 61
Handy, Charles, 61, 63–4
Harvard Business School, 10, 48, 86
Harvey-Jones, (Sir) John, 61
Hawkes, John, 168n26
Hay McBer, 133
Heller, Joseph, 177n4
Hertfordshire Police Force, 15
Hertz, Noreena, 199n16
Hewitt, Bob, 140n34
Higher Education Funding Council for England, 44–5
Hitler, Adolf, 107, 158, 180n8
Henley College, 82
Heseltine, (Lord) Michael, 16n9
H. M. Prisons, 24, 43–4, 48
Hoggart, Richard, 24
Hong Kong, 193
Hopwood, Anthony, 86
Horton, (Sir) Robert, 195
Howarth, Alan, 99
Hull Education Authority, 31–2
Hull, University of, 148
Hutton, Will, 93n31, 155–6
Huxley, Aldous, 177–8

India, 194
Ingrams, Richard, 195n7
"issuing guidelines", 19n12, 23

Jamiroquai, 110
Jeffcutt, Paul, 60n13
Jenkins, Rt. Rev'd David, 45
Jenkins, Simon, 163–4
John, (Sir) Elton, 110
Johnson, Harry, 80
Johnson, Nevil, 196n9
Jones, Donald G., 151, 152n19
Joseph, (Sir) Keith, 123–5
Jowell, Tessa, 19n12, 203

Kadish, Alon, 192

Kaiser, Michael, 115
Kallinikos, J. 76n8
Kay, John, 85–6
Keating's Australian Government, 106
Kent Police, 58–9
Kingston, University of, 82
Kydd, Lesley, 119n3

Lancaster, University of, 82
Lawrence, D. H., 174–7
Law Society, 16
Leeds, University of, 82
Leicester, 169
Leicester–Loughborough Railway, 36
Leicester, University of, 82
Lincolnshire and Humberside University, 88–9
Liverpool John Moores University, 87
"local management of schools", 125
Locke, Robert R., 10, 11, 85
Lodge, David, 185–6
London Business School, 84
London Dungeon, 167
London, University of, 10, 82, 100
Luton, University of, 86

Mackay, Charles, 198, 203
Mackintosh, (Sir) Cameron, 163
Manchester Metropolitan University, 82
Manchester, University of, 11
Mandelson, Peter, 12, 160–3
Manet, Edouard, 92
Marks, Steven, 38
Marshall, Steven, 195
Marxism, 202–3
Massachussets Institute of Technology, 26
McDonalds UK, 168–9
McGregor, Douglas, 130n17
McLure, Stuart, 127
Mead, Richard, 65–6
Methodism, 14–23, 148–52
Meeting the Challenge of Change, 120

Menwith Hills Signals Intelligence Unit, 20
Michigan School of Administration, 10
Micklethwaite, John, and Wooldridge, Adrian, 10n3
Millennium Dome, 161–7, 169–70
Millett, Trevor, 34
Mills, Bertram, 34
Mintzberg, Henry, 32, 79
Morris, John, 174
Morris, Estelle, 129
Morrison, Richard, 164–5
Motion, (Sir) Andrew, 11n5, 99
Mouzelis, N. P., 146n10
"multi–culturalism", 40n13, 169
Murdoch, Rupert, 106
Museums and Galleries Association/Commission, 99, 103, 167
Museums, Libraries and Archives Council, 167
Mussolini's Italy, 103
Mutch, A., 76n8

Naisbitt, John, 60
National Arts and Media Strategy, 100–1
National Audit Office, 17
National Centre for Popular Music, Sheffield, 113, 193
National Curriculum, 119, 124, 126–7
National Front, East Midlands Branch, 17
National Grid for Learning, 137
National Health Service, 16–7, 47, 195
National Lottery, 22, 106–7, 113
National Trust, 50
Natwest Financial Literacy Centre for Education and Industry, Warwick, 135
NESTA, 110–1, 113
New Local Authorities: Management and Structure, The, 20–1
New Millennium Experience Co., 166

New Opportunities Fund, 113
Nightingale, Florence, 13
"Non–Departmental   Public
    Bodies", 22, 24
Norris, Christopher, 177n5
North London University, 82
Nottinghamshire Rural Com-
    munity Council, 55
Nottingham, University of, 82
Nutravida, 33–4

Oasis, 110
Office of Arts and Libraries, 99,
    103,105
OFSTED, 129, 131, 139
Oldham, 99
Olivier, Richard, 173
Olympics, 158
Orwell, George, 157, 179–80
Oswald, Andrew and Gardner,
    Jonathan, 43n16
"outcomes", 42, 91, 163, 194
Oxford, University of, 24, 85–6,
    123

Page, Jennie, 10n1, 164–6
Palethorpe's Sausages, 33
Pavlov, Ivan, 178
Pearce, David, 178n6
Personal   Finance   Education
    Group, 135
Peters, Tom, 60, 62
Pick, John, 101–2
Piercy, Nigel, 84
Policy for the Arts: the First Steps , 96
Policy Studies Institute, 53, 99–
    100
Pollard, Arthur, 174n4
Pritchard, Craig, 90, 204n25
"proactive", 22
Prodigy, The, 110
Pro-Share, 135
Protherough, Robert, 116, 76n8,
    116n12
Pugh, Derek, 70n2

Quality Assurance Agency, 91

Quelch, John, 84

Railtrack, 33n6, 166, 193–5
Ramsbotham, (Sir) David, 43n17
Ranson, Stewart, Bryman, Alan
    and Hinings, Bob, 153n20
Rea, Ernie, 150
Reckitt's Dyes, 33
Rees-Mogg, (Lord) William, 23
Regional Sports Board for the
    South East, 159
*Report of the Consultative Committee
    on Examinations in Secondary
    Schools*, 122n5
Resource, 167
Resourcing Bishops, 196n11
Reynolds, Fiona, 50n1
Reynolds, (Sir) Joshua, 95
Robin Hood Experience, 167
Robinson, John, 144
Rolls-Royce, 34
Roman Catholic Church, 144, 149
Rose, H. B., 72n3, 73
Rowntrees, the Joseph, 13
Royal Academy, 109
Royal National Theatre, 48, 107
Royal Opera House, 114–5
RSC, 39

Said, Wafic, 85
Scruton, Roger, 161
Seabrook. John, 72n2
Seal, 110
Selwood, Sara, 47n4
Shakespeare, William, 40n13, 53,
    92, 173, 178–9
Shaw, Mike, 169
Sheffield City Council, 112
Sheffield, University of, 82
Shipham's Paste, 38
Short White Paper on Entering
    the E.E.C., 19–20
Showalter, Elaine, 199
Smith,   Chris,   45,   98,   105n7,
    107–11, 114, 158, 160–3, 202
Smithers, Alan, 134n20
Smith, W. H., 13

Solzhenitsyn, Aleksandr, 180n3
Sorrell, Martin, 56
Southam, Hazel, 141n4
Southern, Terry, 186
Spalding, Julian, 203
Spice Girls, 110
Spong, Jack, 141n3
Stanford University, 86
"step change", 162
Stone, Maria Susan, 103n5
Straw, Jack, 25n18
Stewart, Rosemary, 77
Sutherland, Keith, 196n8

Tates Britain and Modern, 29,
  54, 168n25, 170
Taylor, Frederick Winslow, 9, 15,
  177
*Teaching of English in Secondary
  Schools, The*, 122n5
Teaching Quality, 124n6
Thames Valley University, 82
Thatcher, (Lady) Margaret, 16,
  21–2, 96–7
Theatres Report 1892, 39–40
Third Reich, The, 103, 107, 158,
  204
Thomas, A. B. and Anthony, P. B.,
  76n8
Thomas, Keith, 199
Thompson, Kenneth A., 153n21
Thoreau, Henry, 18
Timothy White's, 38
"total quality management", 90–1
Towery, Twyman, 62
Toynbee, Polly, 141
Training and Enterprise Councils,
  196
Tusa, John, 197

UB40, 110
Urban Development Corpor-
  ations, 195–6
USA, 10–11, 87, 95, 193
USSR, viii, 22, 23, 103, 107, 130,
  158, 201
Urwick Committee, 73

Vincent, John, 148n13
Vonnegut, Kurt, 180–2

Wade, Graham, 83
"war" on Want/Drugs/Terror-
  ism, 171n30
Warwick, University of, 82, 135
Wells, H. G., 178
Wharton School of Finance and
  Commerce, 10, 85
Whitaker, Patrick, 117n1
White, Joseph B., 92
Whitley, Richard, 72n5
Whitney, John and Packer, Tina,
  173n2
Whyte, William H., 85
Williams, Raymond, 95–6,
Wilson, (Sir) Richard, 24
Wedgwood, Josiah, 34
Woodhead, Chris, 129, 131
Woods, Tiger, 193n4
Wright, Nigel, 128